THE ——
LOOTING
OF SOCIAL
SECURITY

How the Government is Draining
America's Retirement Account

Allen W. Smith, Ph.D.

CARROLL & GRAF PUBLISHERS
NEW YORK

THE LOOTING OF SOCIAL SECURITY

Carroll & Graf Publishers
An Imprint of Avalon Publishing Group Inc.
245 West 17th Street
11th Floor
New York, NY 10011

Library of Congress Cataloging-in-Publication Data is available.

ISBN: 0-7867-1281-3

Designed by Kathleen Lake, Neuwirth and Associates, Inc.

Printed in the United States of America
Distributed by Publishers Group West

For my wife,
Joan Rugel Smith

and family,
Mark, Jacki, and Connor,
Michael,
Lisa and Gary
Grandma, Inez W. Smith

~

Contents

❧

Tables

～

Social Security Chronology

~

1935   Original Social Security Legislation providing for payments to retired employees age 65 or over covered under the system. Social Security funds were to be kept separate from general revenue funds. Payments made into the system were to be credited to accounts for the individuals who had paid them.

1939   Survivors' benefits added to Social Security.

1956   Disability benefits added to Social Security.

        Minimum retirement age for women decreased from 65 years to 62, with decreased benefits.

1961   Minimum retirement age for men decreased from 65 to 62, with decreased benefits.

1965   Medicare added to Social Security.

1969   Johnson administration begins counting Social Security funds in the federal budget.

1974   With passage of the Congressional Budget and Impoundment Control Act, Congress adopts a process for developing budget goals that officially count Social Security as part of the unified budget.

1976– Small annual deficits occur in the Social Security fund.
1982

1982   Greenspan National Commission recommends that the operations of the Social Security trust fund be removed from the unified budget, restoring its pre-1969 status.

       Greenspan Commission recommends legislation that would increase Social Security payroll taxes in order to build up the fund in preparation for the baby-boomer retirement surge beginning 2010.

1983   Recommendations of Greenspan Commission that Social Security taxes be raised to ensure solvency of the reserve fund after 2010 are enacted into law. Revenue from the Social Security payroll tax to be used for Social Security and for Social Security alone.

1983– Gradual increase in annual Social Security surpluses.
1988

1989   Social Security surplus exceeds $50 billion for the first time, and government use of Social Security money for non-Social Security purposes begins to become a controversial political issue.

1990   Senator Daniel Patrick Moynihan proposes that Social Security taxes be cut, and the "pay-as-you-go" system be restored so that there will be no surplus funds to tempt poaching politicians.

The Budget Enforcement Act of 1990 becomes law. It removes the income and outgo of the Social Security trust fund from all calculations of the federal budget, including the budget deficit or surplus. This law made it illegal to include Social Security in the federal budget or to use it in calculating budget deficits or surpluses.

1998   President Clinton announces a $69.2 billion budget surplus when in fact the government runs a $30 billion on-budget deficit. Clinton simply subtracted the $30 billion operating budget deficit from the planned temporary Social Security surplus of $99.2 billion and declared the first budget surplus since the Vietnam War. This was the beginning of the infamous budget-surplus myth that would be used to confuse and deceive the public for the next three years.

1999   President Clinton announces the first true budget surplus (excluding Social Security) in 40 years. The on-budget surplus was $1.9 billion.

2000   Second Clinton true budget surplus. The government ran an $86.6 billion on-budget surplus.

2001   President George W. Bush pushes through a $1.35 trillion ten-year tax cut based on his assertion that the government has massive amounts of surplus money, not counting the Social Security surplus.

The on-budget deficit for President Bush's first year in office is $33.5 billion.

2002   The on-budget deficit soars to $261.7 billion during Bush's second year in office.

2003   President George W. Bush pushes through an additional tax cut of $350 billion despite a petition against it signed by more than 400 of the nation's top economists, including 10 winners of the Nobel prize in economics.

The Bush administration's Office of Management and Budget (OMB) releases a report in July acknowledging the ballooning deficit. The report estimates a unified budget deficit of $455 billion for fiscal year 2003. This translates into an estimated on-budget deficit of more than $600 billion for the year.

2010   The baby-boom generation will begin to retire causing a surge in Social Security benefit payments.

2018   Social Security benefits are expected to exceed Social Security revenue, and from that point on there will be growing annual budget deficits in the Social Security trust fund.

2042   The Social Security trust fund is expected to go broke, even if the government has repaid all the funds it has borrowed from Social Security over the decades. This means that, although the Social Security program will continue to receive revenue, the revenue will not be enough to cover the benefits due, and there will be no reserves left in the trust fund, not even in the form of government IOUs. It is estimated that the revenue during 2042 would be enough to pay approximately 72 percent of the benefits due that year. The situation would then deteriorate annually from that point on.

THE
LOOTING
OF SOCIAL
SECURITY

~

CHAPTER ONE

An Overview

~

No more easy money for corporate criminals. Just hard time. This law says to every dishonest corporate leader, you'll be exposed and punished. The era of low standards and false profits are over.

—President George W. Bush, [July 30, 2002]

*P*RESIDENT GEORGE W. BUSH promised to lead the charge against corporate fraud when it was discovered by financial regulators and a few investigative journalists that Enron, WorldCom, and several other major companies were bilking stockholders. He claimed that his administration would show no mercy for the "corporate wrongdoers." However, Bush's hard-line stand was seen by many as hypocritical on two counts. First of all, although Enron's practices had worried some regulators for a long time before the scandal came to light, the Bush administration had taken no action. Enron CEO, Ken Lay, had actually been one of Bush's biggest financial contributors, donating nearly $2 million to Bush campaigns.

Second, President Bush, the CEO of the largest firm in the world, is himself participating in massive illegal fraud against the American public, much like his predecessors in office. Enron's game was to conceal debt with accounting tricks. The federal government has been doing precisely that with the Social Security trust fund.

The corporate scandals involve cheating on numbers for short-term economic advantage. The government has been cheating on numbers for short-term political advantage since the mid 1980s. In addition to President George W. Bush, President George Herbert Walker Bush and President Bill Clinton, along with most members of Congress, have been willing participants in this fraud, and the public will ultimately pay a much higher price for this deliberate deception than the price investors are paying for business fraud. Some have even suggested that the way Enron ran its business was closely modeled on the way the Social Security Administration runs its ship.

The Social Security Amendments of 1983 laid the foundation for the worst fiscal fraud in the nation's history, and that fraud is worse today than ever before. The legislation was enacted to improve the solvency of the Social Security trust fund that had run small budget deficits for seven years in a row, from 1976 through 1982. The legislation, which was in response to a recommendation the previous year by a Presidential Commission headed by Alan Greenspan (former economic adviser to President Ford and future Federal Reserve Board Chairman), was designed specifically for the purpose of building up a surplus in the Social Security trust fund in preparation for the staggering new obligations the fund would face when the baby-boom generation begins retiring, about 2010. Both Social Security tax rates and the tax base were gradually raised over a seven-year period so the trust fund would be solvent when it takes the big financial hit that will result from the retirement of the most populous generation in American history.

The Budget Enforcement Act of 1990 requires that Social Security funds be kept separate from general government operating funds, and the two funds are not to be commingled. As a result, the government releases budget-deficit or budget-surplus figures for the two funds separately. The on-budget (or operating) deficit or surplus is the difference between government receipts and expenditures, *excluding the Social Security system.*

For all practical purposes, the off-budget deficit or surplus is the deficit or surplus in the Social Security program. Technically, the United States Postal Service is also legally designated as off-budget.

However, since the Postal Service must maintain an approximately balanced budget in its operations, we can essentially equate the off-budget surplus or deficit with that of the Social Security system. Thus, the on-budget deficit or surplus is a measure of whether the government is operating in the red or in the black, and the off-budget surplus or deficit is a measure of the solvency of the Social Security system.

The 1983 legislation generated a Social Security surplus of $9.4 billion in 1985 with increasingly larger annual surpluses thereafter. The Social Security surplus was $38.8 billion in 1988, $56.6 billion in 1990, and $99.2 billion in 1998. Ironically, it was that 1998 Social Security surplus that paved the way for the greatest deception of all.

That year the government ran a deficit of $30.0 billion in the non-Social Security budget. However, since the Social Security surplus was larger than the operating-budget (on-budget) deficit for the first time ever, President Clinton took a giant leap into fantasyland and announced that the government had a surplus of $69.2 billion, the first surplus since the Vietnam War.

President Clinton's claim that the United States government had a $69.2 billion surplus in 1998, when in fact the government spent $30 billion more than its non-Social Security revenue, amounted to a greater fraud against the American people than any of the deceptive practices of the so-called "corporate wrongdoers."

The American people have been told over and over that their Social Security taxes go into a trust fund where reserves are kept to pay for future retirement benefits. That is a lie! Not a penny of anybody's Social Security taxes ever goes into a special fund for purposes of paying benefits at some point in the future. Every year, all Social Security tax receipts collected are spent during that same year by the government. Whatever is left over after paying the benefits is spent by the government on other programs, or used to finance tax cuts. Absolutely none of the tax receipts are reserved for paying future retirement benefits.

In fact, the Social Security system is being run like a giant illegal

Ponzi scheme. For those not familiar with the terminology, the U.S. Securities and Exchange Commission defines "Ponzi" schemes on its official website as follows:

> Ponzi schemes are a type of illegal pyramid scheme named for Charles Ponzi, who duped thousands of New England residents into investing in a postage stamp speculation scheme back in the 1920s. . . . Ponzi told investors that he could provide a 40% return in just 90 days . . . Ponzi was deluged with funds from investors, taking in $1 million during one three-hour period—and this was 1921! . . .
>
> Decades later, the Ponzi scheme continues to work on the "rob-Peter-to-pay-Paul" principle, as money from new investors is used to pay off earlier investors until the whole scheme collapses.

The second paragraph of the preceding quotation from the Securities and Exchange Commission is a perfect description of how the Social Security system is run today. The "money from new investors" (workers currently paying payroll taxes into the fund) is used to pay off "earlier investors" (retired workers who paid into the system in the past, but whose benefits are being paid from the contributions collected from current workers) "until the whole scheme collapses."

Although the Social Security trust fund has been running surpluses in recent years because of the 1983 increases in the Social Security payroll taxes, shortly after the baby boomers begin retiring, about 2010, the fund will begin to run deficits. In 2018 the annual benefits payments are expected to exceed the annual revenue, and the Social Security deficit will widen with each passing year after that.

There will, of course, continue to be the fantasy reserves in the form of government IOUs, but you can't pay benefits with nonmarketable federal government IOUs. As early as 1989, Senator Ernest (Fritz) Hollings (D-SC) predicted that these IOUs would become the twenty-first century version of worthless Confederate banknotes. All that these IOUs represent is an accounting of how much money has been "embezzled" from the Social Security trust fund by the government.

The IOUs are supposed to represent an obligation of the federal government to repay the "borrowed" money. But when push comes to shove, I'm betting that politicians will opt for slashing Social Security benefits instead of increasing taxes to raise the money needed to repay its debt to the Social Security system. Tomorrow's politicians will blame yesterday's politicians for misusing the funds and will argue that they should not have to raise taxes or take other politically unpopular actions because of the irresponsible actions of previous office-holders. Most politicians will come out smelling like a rose, despite the awful stench assaulting the masses of Americans who will have been betrayed by their own government.

The most likely scenario is that Social Security will become a "means tested" welfare program with benefits available only to the very poor. All those people who have paid into the fund, if they are not poor, will have been swindled out of their contributions. When that time comes, it will make the Enron scandal look like a lemonade stand bankruptcy.

Paul O'Neill, Treasury Secretary from 2001-2003, referred to the newly passed "corporate reform" legislation as a "lock on the barn door," to prevent the kind of corporate misdeeds that had shaken investors' confidence.

The "lock on the barn door" analogy had a hollow ring to it for those people who remembered the Social Security "lockbox" debate during the 2000 election campaign and President Bush's broken promise to not touch Social Security funds for any purpose other than to pay Social Security benefits. And to those who understood that, like his predecessors, Bush is continuing to operate the Social Security program like a giant illegal Ponzi scheme, it seemed that Bush's tough words for corporate "wrongdoers" should be applied to the President himself.

Despite the legal requirement that operating funds and Social

Security funds be kept separate, the government has devised a misleading measure called the "unified budget," which combines the two budget categories. By combining the two funds, a large surplus in the Social Security budget can more than offset the on-budget (operating) deficit and show a surplus in the unified budget. This is the primary trick that the government has been using to deceive the public into believing there is a surplus in the operating budget when there is none.

The Office of Management and Budget (OMB), a division of the Executive Office of The President of the United States, publishes "A Citizen's Guide to the Federal Budget." Among the revelations of this official publication is the following statement:

> When the unified budget first booked a surplus of $69 billion in 1998, the on-budget accounts were still in deficit by $30 billion. In 1999, the unified budget ran a $124 billion surplus, nearly all of which was the result of the Social Security surplus. The on-budget accounts were almost exactly in balance.

Thus even the Executive Office of the President of the United States verifies that the only place there was a surplus was in the Social Security trust fund! Yet, on June 26, 2000, President Clinton announced a projected surplus of $1.9 trillion over the next decade. The announcement was made in such a way as to lead journalists to believe he was talking about a surplus in the operating budget. Below is a sample (from ABC News.com) of the way this story was reported to the public.

> WASHINGTON, June 26—Flush with cash from the soaring economy, the U.S. government has even more money to spend than was tthought just a few months ago. President Clinton announced today that over the next decade, the federal budget surplus will total nearly $1.9 trillion. That's more than 2 $1/2$ times what the administration predicted it would be in February.

"The American people should be very proud of this news," Clinton
said as he announced the new numbers in the Rose Garden this after-
noon. "It's the result of their hard work and their support for fiscal discipline. It's proof that we can create a better future for ourselves when
we put our minds to it."

.... But even as the president hailed the new numbers, he cautioned
against making plans to spend all of the projected tax revenue.

"This is just a budget projection," he said. "It would not be prudent
to commit every penny of a future surplus that is just a projection and
therefore subject to change." . . .

"It would be a big mistake to commit this entire surplus to spending or tax cuts," Clinton said . . . "The projections could be wrong, they
could be right."

President Clinton did the country a great disservice with that
announcement. He knew how it would be interpreted by the media,
and his motives for making it were exclusively political. After eight
years of dealing with budget figures, he had to know that the projections were phony. He also knew that whatever the size of any budget
surpluses over the next decade, almost all of the money would belong
to the Social Security program.

President Clinton initially created the budget-surplus myth in
1998. However, it was George W. Bush who has used the myth most
extensively in his effort to deceive the American people as to the true
status of the federal budget. The alleged budget surplus was almost
like a gift from the gods to Governor Bush, who had pinned almost
all his hopes for making it to the White House on selling his big proposed tax cut to the public. Just such a tax cut had propelled Ronald
Reagan into the White House, and Bush was going to attempt to ride
the same horse into the oval office.

There was, however, a major problem with Bush's plan. Americans
were wary about going down the Reaganomics road again because the
Reagan tax cut had produced massive deficits and quadrupled the
national debt in just 12 years. The deficit problem resulting from

Reaganomics was reversed only after the enactment of the Clinton deficit-reduction package. (Reaganomics is covered in chapter 4.)

Clinton provided a solution to Bush's problem by creating the budget surplus myth and convincing the American people that huge budget surpluses loomed ahead as far as the eye could see. However, Clinton did at least warn against using the projected surpluses.

Bush took the position that the alleged budget surpluses were the result of overtaxing the American people, and claimed,

> The surplus money belongs to the American taxpayers—not to the government—and it should be returned to the people in the form of a tax cut.

Bush was wrong on both counts. The money did not belong to the government or the general public. It belonged to the Social Security trust fund and to the hardworking Americans whose payroll-tax contributions created the Social Security surplus. And the surplus in Social Security existed only because of the 1983 Social Security tax increases that were designed specifically for the purpose of building up a temporary surplus in the trust fund in preparation for the retirement of the baby-boom generation.

The 1983 legislation was in direct response to the recommendations of the 1982 Greenspan National Commission on Social Security Reform, and the commission made it very clear that the Social Security program should be kept separate from the general operating budget. The commission report even warned that if the Social Security funds were counted in the unified budget they could have the deceptive effect of making a general budget deficit appear smaller than it actually was. Excerpts from the report of the 1982 Greenspan Commission report follow.

> A majority of the members of the National Commission recommends that the operations of the OASI, DI, HI, and SMI trust funds should be removed from the unified budget . . .

Before fiscal year 1969, the operations of the Social Security trust funds were not included in the unified budget of the Federal Government, although they were made available publicly and were combined, for purposes of economic analysis, with the administrative budget in special summary tables included in the annual budget document.

Beginning then, the operations of the Social Security trust funds were included in the unified budget. . . . Thus, in years when trust-fund income exceeded outgo, the result was a decrease in any general budget deficit that otherwise would have been shown . . .

The same ABC News.com article that was quoted earlier also reported the reaction of the Bush camp to President Clinton's announcement of the huge projected surplus.

Today's report confirms the accuracy of the conservative estimates Governor Bush used in preparing his balanced budget plan," said Bush spokesman Ari Fleischer. "The report also demonstrates the importance of passing the governor's tax cuts to prevent all this new money from being spent on bigger government.

Did Governor Bush really believe there was any new money except that resulting from the higher Social Security taxes that were specifically earmarked for retirement funding after 2010? The United States government had more than $4.5 trillion in unpaid bills just from the previous 20 years of excess spending.

Surely the younger Bush knew that his father's administration had spent $1.1 trillion more than it collected in revenue during President Bush's four-year term. Why wasn't George W. Bush trying to find ways to undo the damage done during the Reagan-Bush years by paying down at least part of the debt accumulated during those years of irresponsible deficit spending? If he truly understood the government's financial condition, why would he call for additional tax cuts?

*   *   *

IT WAS BUSH'S FATHER, the "read-my-lips-no-new-taxes" president, who had set the precedent for using Social Security dollars to fund other government programs. The Social Security trust fund ran surpluses totaling $211.7 billion during Bush's four-year term, and Bush spent every dollar of the surplus funds on other government programs. He ran average annual on-budget (operating budget) deficits of more than $286 billion per year, and the national debt that had been only $1 trillion at the beginning of the Reagan-Bush years, had soared above the $4 trillion mark by the time Bush left office twelve years later.

President George Herbert Walker Bush followed one of the most irresponsible fiscal polices in the nation's history. However, in his effort to deceive the American people, he radiated innocence and good intentions. He tried to persuade the public that he cared deeply about the nation's financial future while he was undermining it through accounting trickery and other maneuvers.

On the evening of October 2, 1990, President George Bush went on national television in an attempt to persuade the public to pressure their representatives in Congress to vote for a proposed budget that Senator Fritz Hollings (D-SC) described as "the worst budget document I have ever seen." The following excerpts are from the President's speech.

Tonight, I want to talk to you about a problem that has lingered and dogged and vexed this country for far too long: the federal budget deficit. Thomas Paine said many years ago, "These are the times that try men's souls." As we speak, our nation is standing together against Saddam Hussein's aggression. But here at home, there is another threat, a cancer gnawing away at our nation's health. That cancer is the budget deficit. Year after year, it mortgages the future of our children.

No family, no nation, can continue to do business the way the federal government has been operating and survive. When you get a bill, that bill must be paid, and when you write a check, you're supposed to have money in the bank. But if you don't obey these simple rules of common sense, there is a price to pay. But for too long, the nation's business in Washington has been conducted as if these basic rules did not apply. Well, these rules do apply. And if we fail to act, next year alone we will face a federal budget deficit of more than $300 billion, a deficit that could weaken our economy further and cost us thousands of precious jobs.

. . . This is the first time in my presidency that I have made an appeal like this to you, the American people. With your help we can at last put this budget crisis behind us and face the other challenges that lie ahead. If we do, the long-term result will be a healthier nation and something more. We will have once again put ourselves on the path of economic growth and we will have demonstrated that no challenge is greater than the determination of the American people.

Thank you, God bless you and good night.

The speech was a superb reminder of the basic rules that apply to sound fiscal management for individuals, businesses, and the government. It is hard to imagine any American not agreeing with the words in this speech. It sure sounded like the president was concerned about the nation's financial future, and he appeared to be against mortgaging our children's economic future. How could we fail to support policies with such noble goals, if we assumed he was being sincere and honest with the American people?

That's the catch: The president was saying one thing and doing something very different. He was trying to convince the public that his policies would lead to an outcome that would be for the common good—one that almost everyone could agree on—when, in reality, he was doing just the opposite.

The following day, Senator Hollings rose on the Senate floor and requested that the President's speech be printed in full in the Congressional Record. There being no objection, the material was ordered to be printed in the Record.

Then Senator Hollings gave his assessment of the proposed budget bill.

. . . It is supposed to solve the deficit problem. Instead it adds $1.2 trillion to the national debt over the 5-year period. That is using the figures given to us by Director Richard Darman of the Office of Management and Budget. Indeed this agreement expressly abandons any pretense of trying to eliminate the deficits. Instead, it talks about "proposed savings." . . . There is no serious deficit reduction purpose. There is a serious purpose of deceit and fraud upon the American people. . . .

. . . I can tell you here and now this is the worst budget document I have ever seen gliding through this body. . . . I fought on this floor against Kemp-Roth, Reaganomics, which George Herbert Walker Bush called voodoo economics. Now he is a high priest of voodoo, a national distributor of voodoo last night on TV, I can tell you that.

The whole issue of government misappropriation of Social Security money came to a head in 1990 when Senator Daniel Patrick Moynihan (D-NY) sent shock waves throughout Washington and much of the nation with his proposal to cut Social Security taxes. Senator Moynihan, who had been a strong supporter of the 1983 efforts to strengthen the Social Security system, was outraged that, instead of being used to build up the size of the Social Security trust fund for future retirees as was intended, the Social Security surplus was being used to pay for general government spending.

Because Moynihan believed the American people were being betrayed and deceived, he proposed undoing the 1983 legislation by cutting Social Security taxes and putting the system back on a "pay-as-you-go" basis, which would have provided only enough revenue to take care of current retirees. Moynihan's position was that if the government could not keep its hands out of the Social Security cookie jar, the jar should be emptied so there would be no Social Security surplus for presidents and Congress to poach.

In response to reporters' questions about Senator Moynihan's proposal to cut Social Security taxes, President Bush replied, "It is an effort to get me to raise taxes on the American people by the charade of cutting them, or cut benefits, and I am not going to do it to the older people of this country."

But President Bush was in fact taking money from a fund that was supposed to be used to provide for "the older people of this country" and spending it on general government operations. Since none of the $211.7 billion borrowed from Social Security by the Bush administration was repaid during the Bush presidency, he left office having ensured that higher taxes will have to be levied against the American people at some point in the future if this debt to Social Security claimants is ever to be repaid.

PRESIDENT GEORGE BUSH continued a practice that had begun in a small way during the second Reagan term and has continued through the Clinton and George W. Bush presidencies. That practice is to spend the dollars generated by Social Security taxes just like any other taxes, even though the Budget Enforcement Act of 1990 mandated that Social Security funds be kept separate from other funds.

Earlier presidents did not have an opportunity to deceive the American people in this way. Even during the first four years of the Reagan administration, the Social Security system ran a net deficit of $12.4 billion. Only during the second Reagan term, and after, did it become possible for elected officials to misappropriate planned Social Security surpluses resulting from the Social Security Amendments of 1983, specifically earmarked to maintain Social Security solvency after 2010.

One of the reasons that it has been so easy for government officials to deceive the American people about the true financial condition of the United States Government is the fact that all Social Security surplus funds are, by law, required to be invested in U.S. Treasury securities. Under current law, the Social Security funds cannot be invested in stocks or bonds.

However, this requirement does not in any way necessitate or justify the use of surplus Social Security funds to finance general government operations. Every dollar of Social Security revenue, in excess of what is required to pay current benefits, would be better used in paying down the gigantic national debt. Doing so would have the equivalent effect of putting the money into a separate bank account that is off limits to politicians who are tempted to borrow the funds to pay for general government operations or to fund tax cuts. Using Social Security surplus funds to pay down the national debt during the Social Security surplus years between now and 2018, and then borrowing those dollars back during the years in which Social Security deficits will occur (after 2018) would be the fiscally responsible thing to do.

IN 2001, PRESIDENT GEORGE W. BUSH sold his huge $1.35 trillion, ten-year tax cut to Congress and the American people by claiming that it would be financed by surplus tax dollars. Furthermore, he promised that he would not take any additional money from Social Security.

In an address to a joint session of Congress on February 27, 2001 Bush said,

> To make sure the retirement savings of America's seniors are not diverted into any other program, my budget protects all $2.6 trillion of the Social Security surplus for Social Security and for Social Security alone.

The next day the Office of Management and Budget released the following statement.

> None of the Social Security trust funds and Medicare trust funds will be used to fund other spending initiatives or tax relief.

A month later, Bush reassured the public that, even with an economic slowdown, his budget was conservative enough to protect the trust funds. In a speech at Western Michigan University on March 27, 2001, the President said,

Tax relief is central to my plan to encourage economic growth, and we can proceed with tax relief without fear of budget deficits, even if the economy softens. Projections for the surplus in my budget are cautious and conservative. They already assume an economic slowdown in the year 2001.

Yet President George W. Bush and his advisers had no intention of reserving any Social Security funds for future benefit payments. They knew there was little likelihood that there would be any non-Social Security surpluses during the Bush presidency. The tiny non-Social Security surplus of $1.9 billion in 1999, and the more substantial $86.6 billion surplus in 2000, during the Clinton administration, had come at a time when the economy was at the peak of the business cycle, with the unemployment rate at a 30-year low, and these two surpluses were the only non-Social Security surpluses in the past 40 years. So how could any reasonable person expect to see continued non-Social Security surpluses once the economy passed the peak of the business cycle?

As it turned out, the Bush administration ran actual non-Social Security deficits of $33.4 billion in fiscal 2001 and $317.5 billion in 2002. Deficits for the next several years are projected to be in excess of $500 billion per year!

The Bush people used accounting trickery and pie-in-the-sky promises to sell the tax cut, knowing that despite the President's public pledge to the American people in his February 27, 2001, address to protect Social Security they would soon be borrowing additional dollars from the Social Security trust fund.

The whopping $317.5 billion non-Social Security deficit in 2002 required the government to borrow all the Social Security surplus and then borrow still more from the public by issuing additional Treasury securities. Furthermore, huge annual non-Social Security deficits, in the range of $400-600 billion, lie ahead as far as the eye can see—and they do not include the cost of the war against Iraq.

If Bush had admitted that he would be using Social Security

payroll-tax receipts, paid by future retirees, to replace the lost revenue resulting from his tax cut that goes mostly to the super rich, the tax bill would not have stood a chance of passing, and he knew it. This deliberate deception of the American public in order to give tax breaks to the class of people who provided him with so much campaign money puts him in the same company as those he so forcefully denounces as "corporate wrongdoers."

Even more reckless than the 2001 tax cut was the $350 billion tax cut pushed through Congress and down the throats of the American people in May 2003 by President George W. Bush. By early 2003, it was quite clear just how wrong Bush had been two years earlier. On top of the $317.5 billion deficit for 2002, a $467.6 billion deficit was being projected for fiscal 2003. The economy had stalled, the unemployment rate had risen to 6 percent, and two million jobs had been lost just since Bush took office. Obviously, the $1.35 trillion tax cut of 2001 had affected the economy very differently than Bush had predicted it would.

So what kind of medicine did the economy need in 2003? According to Bush, we needed still more tax cuts, so in early 2003 he called for a large new tax-cut package, including elimination of the tax on dividend income. Most economists were stunned. Bush was calling for more of the same medicine that had already hurt the economy and the budget so badly.

Professional economists felt so strongly about the threat posed by Bush's latest proposal that more than 400 of the nation's top economists, including 10 Nobel Laureates, signed a statement opposing the tax cut and placed a full-page ad in the *New York Times* to warn the public, and the President, about the dangers of such action.

But President Bush defiantly ignored the economists. He campaigned against them and anyone else who opposed his latest tax cut proposal, and he traveled around America trying to convince the American public to put pressure on Congress to pass it.

On the very same day, May 23, 2003, that the United States Senate passed the tax-cut proposal, only with the tie-breaking vote of

Vice President Cheney, the Senate also voted to raise the national debt ceiling by nearly $1 trillion. This was necessary because the Treasury Department was expected to run out of borrowing authority in less than a week, and risk defaulting on the nation's debt. Historians will have great difficulty understanding how any responsible government official could reduce the government's future income by $350 billion, with an unaffordable tax cut, when the government was less than a week from defaulting on its massive debt unless it got a credit extension from Congress.

George W. Bush, Bill Clinton, and George H. W. Bush have spent every dollar of the approximately $1.5 trillion Social Security surplus resulting from the 1983 Social Security tax increase Americans thought they were paying only to fund the retirement of the baby boomers. Historians will almost certainly condemn all three men for this fraud against the American public.

The temporary Social Security surpluses generated by the 1983 tax hike would never have existed without the 1983 amendments to the Social Security Act, and every penny will eventually be needed to pay Social Security benefits. Will future government leaders raise taxes in order to repay the borrowed money, or will they make massive cuts in Social Security benefits and perhaps even deny benefits to anyone whose income is above a certain level?

Most Americans are totally unaware that not a single dollar of the Social Security taxes they pay each year goes into a trust fund to pay future retirement benefits, either to them or to anyone else. Every dollar of Social Security taxes collected in any given year is also spent during that year. Funds are used first to pay current Social Security benefits to retirees. Even the benefits of people who retired 20 years ago are paid from this year's Social Security tax receipts because that is the only source of funds available for such payments. Once this year's Social Security benefits are paid, any remaining revenue from Social Security taxes goes into the general fund and is spent on whatever the Congress and the president choose to spend it on. It may go for pork-barrel projects, national defense, or to fund tax cuts for the rich.

Social Security payroll taxes paid by American workers are being rerouted to tax cuts for the wealthiest Americans despite the fact that Bush pledged in speech after speech not one dollar of Social Security money would be used to fund either the tax cut or other spending programs.

The Social Security trust fund was always supposed to be kept separate from the general operating budget, but it was not until passage of the Budget Enforcement Act of 1990 that there was an actual federal law prohibiting commingling the two funds. In a speech on the floor of the United States Senate on October 13, 1989, Senator Hollings, a primary sponsor of the 1990 legislation, expressed his outrage at the fraudulent practices that had been taking place. The entire text of the speech is reproduced below from the Congressional Record {Page: S13411}

Mr. HOLLINGS. Mr. President, this morning I joined with the distinguished majority leader, Senator Mitchel, and others to unveil our proposal for taking the Social Security surpluses off budget for purposes of calculating compliance with Gramm-Rudman-Hollings. This leadership initiative will be a critical first step toward restoring truth in Federal budgeting. And, let's face it, until we acknowledge the truth—the scale and enormity—of our deficits, then we will continue on our current wreckless course of do-nothingism, denial and deception.

The late John Mitchell, when he was Attorney General in the Nixon administration, used to say over and over again, "Watch what we do, not what we say." Well, the American people would do well to take that same advice if they want to understand just how desperate our current fiscal crisis really is.

Look not at what we are saying, but at what we are doing. We say that the budget deficit for 1990 will be just under $100 billion. Yet, lo and behold, at the end of this month we are going to raise the debt limit by some 300 billion dollars to allow for expected public borrowing during the fiscal year 1990. Now, if the deficit is only $100 billion, why are we going to borrow $300 billion? The answer is simple. We are going to borrow $300 billion in 1990 because the true deficit, once you cut through all the monkeyshine, is going to be $300 billion. We arrive at that fanciful $100 billion projection only by indulging in enough fraud and larceny and malfeasance to land an ordinary citizen in the penitentiary.

Of course, the most reprehensible fraud in this great jambalaya of frauds is the systematic and total ransacking of the Social Security trust fund in order to mask the true size of the deficit. As we all know, the Social Security payroll tax has become a money machine for the U.S. Treasury, generating fantastic revenue surpluses in excess of the costs of the Social Security program. Excess Social Security tax revenues will be $65 billion in 1990 alone—boosted by yet another rise in the Social Security tax rate, slated to kick in January 1. By 1993, the annual Social Security surplus will soar to $99 billion.

The public fully supported enactment of hefty new Social Security taxes in 1983 to ensure the retirement program's long-term solvency and credibility. The promise was that today's huge surpluses would be set safely aside in a trust fund to provide for baby-boomer retirees in the next century.

Well, look again. The Treasury is siphoning off every dollar of the Social Security surplus to meet current operating expenses of the Government. By thus reducing the deficit, we mask the true enormity of the Federal budget crisis while creating the illusion that Congress and the administration are actually doing something about deficits.

Mr. President, our proposed amendment, which we intend to attach to the debt-ceiling bill, would put Social Security surpluses off budget for purposes of calculating the Federal budget deficit beginning October 1, the first day of fiscal 1990. The distinguished junior Senator from Texas and his Republican colleagues, aiming to rescue the administration's read my lips strategy, plan an alternative amendment that would put Social Security off budget in the distant future, in 1994.

By 1994, however, a cumulative sum, in excess of a half-trillion dollars, will have been borrowed from the Social Security trust fund, and the denuded trust fund will be piled high with IOU's. Those IOU's are a charming bookkeeping nicety, but the sheriff who tries to collect on them is truly going to have his work cut out for him.

The hard fact is that, in the next century, the Social Security system will find itself paying out vastly more in benefits than it is taking in through payroll taxes. And the American people will wake up to the reality that those IOU's in the trust fund vault are a 21st century version of Confederate banknotes.

Of course, the Treasury would have the option of raising taxes to repay the astronomical sums we have borrowed from the trust fund. But that would be a brazen ripoff of working Americans, many of whom will be retirees obliged to pay a second time for the benefits they have already earned.

On the other hand, if the Treasury wimps out and chooses not to raise taxes to reimburse the trust fund, then there will be no alternative but to slash Social Security benefits. The most likely scenario is that Social Security payments would be turned into just another means-tested welfare program for the very poor; if you make more than say, $15,000 per year, then forget about collecting any Social Security benefits.

Any way you slice it, it is a lousy public policy to borrow massively from the Social Security trust fund with no credible plan for reimbursement. Of course, the immediate damage from this approach is that it allows us to mask the true scale of the Federal budget deficit, thus making it easier for us politicians to sit on our hands.

This is a gross breach of faith with the American people. Social Security is perhaps the most successful social program ever enacted by the Federal Government. Without question, it is the most effective antipoverty program in history. Social Security is not charity or welfare. On the contrary, it is a supplementary retirement fund that workers pay for with their hard-earned money.

I say it is time to stop playing games with Social Security and the government's finances. It is time to use honest budget numbers and to make honest budget choices. By all means, let us begin by putting Social Security truly in trust and totally off budget.

Mr. President, I ask unanimous consent that the text of my original bill be printed in the Record at this point.

Senator Hollings' proposal eventually became Section 13301 of the Budget Enforcement Act of 1990, which was signed into law by President Bush on November 5, 1990. It prohibited including Social Security funds in any budget calculations, including deficits or surpluses.

Section 13301 explicitly states:

> Not withstanding any other provision of law, the receipts and disbursements of the Federal Old Age and Survivors Insurance Trust Fund and the Federal Disability Insurance Trust Fund shall not be counted as new budget authority, outlays, receipts, or deficit or surplus for purposes of (1) the budget of the United States Government as submitted by the President, (2) the Congressional budget, or (3) the Balanced Budget and Emergency Deficit Control Act of 1985.

Senator Hollings thought that by making it illegal for the Congress and the president to include Social Security funds in their budget calculations the deliberate deception of the public would come to an end. But he was wrong. The Bush administration and many members of Congress got over this tiny hurdle by simply ignoring the law. They continued their deceptive practices just as they had done before. But there was a difference. Now they were guilty of more than deception. Now they were guilty of deliberately violating federal law.

President Clinton reversed the trend of larger and larger budget deficits. At the beginning of his first term, he pushed through Congress a deficit reduction package which included both tax increases and spending cuts. Republicans opposed this deficit reduction package adamantly because it included higher taxes, and not a single Republican voted for the measure. The bill passed the Senate only by the tie-breaking vote of Vice President Al Gore, and Republicans insisted that the Clinton policy would wreck the economy.

Now, with the benefit of hindsight, we know that the deficits grew smaller and smaller, and the economy grew stronger and stronger throughout the Clinton Presidency. Finally, in 1999, the government experienced the first balanced budget in 40 years. Actually, a tiny surplus of $1.9 billion was reported after several revisions, but it was essentially a balanced budget. In Fiscal 2000, there was a non-Social Security surplus of $86.6 billion at a time that the economy was at the peak of the business cycle with the unemployment rate at a 30-year low.

The tiny surplus of 1999, and the more significant surplus in 2000, were the only true surpluses in the past 40 years. All the talk about surpluses as far as the eye could see was based on phony and fraudulent projections using unrealistic assumptions.

In fiscal 2001 the budget returned to deficit territory with a non-Social Security deficit of $33.4 billion, and in 2002, as we've noted, the deficit soared to $317.5 billion. We face massive deficits in the years ahead. In 2018, the Social Security fund is expected to begin running deficits, in addition to the deficits in the general operating budget. Without radical changes in government policies, the fiscal future of the United States Government looks so bleak that none of us can be sure what catastrophes lie ahead.

It's time to eradicate fraud in the federal government, and make public officials pay the same price for fraud that they are now demanding of corporate "wrongdoers." George W. Bush demanded that the CEOs of all private companies in America follow sound accounting practices and abide by the law. As the CEO of the largest firm in the world, Bush needs to practice what he preaches!

Table 1 shows the non-Social Security surplus or deficit, and the Social Security surplus or deficit, from 1981 through 2003, as well as the public debt at the end of each fiscal year. A tiny Social Security surplus was recorded in 1983, marking the end of seven consecutive years of deficits in the fund and the beginning of the era of Social Security surpluses resulting from the 1983 tax increase. Prior to that time, Social Security had operated on a pay-as-you-go basis with no

TABLE 1

SURPLUSES OR DEFICITS AND PUBLIC DEBT, 1981-2003

(in Billions of Dollars)

Year	Non-Social Security Surplus(+) or Deficit(-)	Social Security Surplus(+) or Deficit(-)	Public Debt End of Fiscal Year
1981	-74.0	-5.0	994.8
1982	-120.1	-7.9	1,137.3
1983	-208.0	+0.2	1,371.7
1984	-185.7	+0.3	1,564.7
1985	-221.7	+9.4	1,817.5
1986	-238.0	+16.7	2,120.6
1987	-169.3	+19.6	2,346.1
1988	-194.0	+38.8	2,601.3
1989	-205.2	+52.8	2,868.0
1990	-277.8	+56.6	3,206.6
1991	-321.6	+52.2	3,598.5
1992	-340.5	+50.1	4,002.1
1993	-300.5	+45.3	4,351.4
1994	-258.9	+55.7	4,643.7
1995	-226.4	+62.4	4,921.0
1996	-174.1	+66.6	5,181.9
1997	-103.4	+81.4	5,369.7
1998	-30.0	+99.2	5,478.7
1999	+1.9	+123.7	5,606.1
2000	+86.6	+149.8	5,629.0
2001	-33.4	+160.7	5,770.3
2002	-317.5	+159.7	6,198.4
2003*	-467.6	+163.5	6,752.0

Source: Economic Report of the President, 2003
*Estimates

large surpluses. This practice worked fine so long as the number of new retirees each year remained relatively stable. Then, the Presidential Commission of 1982 headed by Alan Greenspan noted that beginning in about 2010, there would be such an acceleration in the number of retirees over a period of several years that the trust fund could not possibly remain solvent without massive amounts of new revenue.

In response to the Commission's concerns, Congress sought to gradually build up the fund prior to 2010 by raising taxes gradually over a seven-year period. The surplus for 1985 was $9.4 billion, and by 1990 it had grown to $56.6 billion. By 2001, the Social Security surplus had risen to $160.5 billion.

It should be remembered that these annual surpluses were a part of the blueprint designed to get the fund ready for the baby boomers, and that the fund will again begin to experience annual deficits in about 2018. This money from the temporary surplus years was to be set aside for the specific purpose of keeping the Social Security fund solvent. The plan was to use the Social Security surpluses to pay down the national debt. This would have been like putting the money into a separate bank account, and it could have been borrowed back by the Federal government when it was needed to pay Social Security benefits.

Instead, what government leaders have done is to defy the intent of the 1983 legislation and use the Social Security surplus dollars to pay for other government programs, ultimately helping finance a major tax cut that strongly favors the rich. This practice represented fraud against the American people on a scale unprecedented in American history. The government deliberately deceived the public into believing that the planned Social Security surplus was really a general revenue surplus, and President George W. Bush used this fraud-based public perception to justify enactment of his massive $1.35 trillion tax cut in 2001. As things stand now, it appears that this tax cut for the rich will be paid for primarily with funds generated by the regressive Social Security payroll tax levied on American workers.

With the increase in retirees between 2010 and 2015, Social Security benefit payments will begin to soar, and in about 2018 the Social Security fund is expected to begin running annual deficits. The interest earnings from past surpluses will keep the fund afloat for a while, if the government begins to actually pay interest instead of issuing IOUs, but eventually the government will have to start repaying the principle, plus interest, in order for the fund to remain solvent.

If the government does not fully repay its obligations to the Social Security trust fund, with interest, whenever the funds are needed, benefits will have to be reduced. In addition, the Social Security fund is not actuarially sound on a long-term basis; even if the government repays all it owes with interest. Without reforms, the fund is expected to be broke by about 2042. However, the fund will be in trouble much sooner if the government does not quickly get its act together.

Social Security taxes, like all other government revenues, are deposited in the U.S. Treasury and become part of the government's operating cash pool. Through separate accounting entries, the government keeps a record of how much money is supposed to be in the Social Security trust fund. Similarly, Social Security benefits are paid from the Treasury, not from the trust fund. Essentially, the only way that Social Security receipts and payments are kept separate from other government financing is through bookkeeping entries by the U.S. Treasury.

Government IOUs, called "special issues of the Treasury," are posted to the account of the Social Security trust fund. These "special-issue" securities have no commercial value because they cannot be sold in the marketplace. When Social Security benefits are paid out, a corresponding amount of securities is deducted from the trust fund. In essence, the only thing in the Social Security trust fund is non-marketable government IOUs representing a promise by the government that it will obtain resources in the future equal to the value of the securities whenever such resources are needed to pay Social Security benefits.

These IOUs are supposed to be earning interest, but the government pays the interest on funds borrowed from the Social Security trust fund with non-marketable "special-issue" securities just like the ones posted when the money was borrowed. [*This means that both the assets and the interest earnings of the Social Security trust fund are in the form of government IOUs that have no commercial value.*]

IN SUMMARY, the federal government has been engaging in fraud against the American people ever since passage of the 1983 Social Security amendments. The tax increase was intended to build up a reserve so the Social Security trust fund could remain solvent when it took the big financial hit resulting from the increased number of retirees in 2010 and after.

George Herbert Walker Bush, the "read-my-lips, no-new-taxes" president, spent every dollar of the Social Security surplus on other government programs. President Bill Clinton did the same thing, but he did reduce the deficits from the $340.5 billion during the last year of the George Bush presidency to $30 billion in 1998, after which he ran budget surpluses for his last two years in office.

George W. Bush is now following in the footsteps of his father and Clinton, and spending the entire Social Security surplus—despite his pledge that Social Security funds would be used only for the payment of Social Security benefits. What makes George W. Bush's actions even worse than those of his father and President Clinton, is that he is using Social Security revenue paid by American workers to fund tax cuts that primarily benefit the wealthy.

The government has been deceiving the public into believing the money is still in the Social Security trust fund when:

- There is nothing in the fund except non-marketable government IOUs.
- Every dollar of Social Security revenue received in any given year is spent during that year.
- People who retired 20 years ago are paid benefits from this

year's revenue, and people who retire 10 years from now will
not find any of their contributions still available.

It is only a matter of time until the annual revenue will be insufficient to pay for all the benefits due that year. When that time comes,
something will have to give. Either there will be a substantial tax
increase or benefits will have to be cut.

CHAPTER TWO

The Social Security Trust Fund

~

Let the people know the truth and the country is safe.

—Abraham Lincoln

THE UNITED STATES WAS one of the last advanced nations in the world to establish a social security system. In a speech to Congress on January 17, 1935, President Franklin D. Roosevelt urged passage of the Social Security Act. Roosevelt said, "It is a sound idea—a sound ideal. Most of the other advanced countries of the world have already adopted it and their experience affords the knowledge that social insurance can be made a sound and workable project."

President Roosevelt stressed the importance of developing a "self-sustaining" system under which funds would be separate from general government financing. He said, "The system adopted, except for the money necessary to initiate it, should be self-sustaining in the sense that funds for the payment of insurance benefits should not come from the proceeds of general taxation."

With passage of the Social Security Act of 1935, America joined the rest of the developed world in making a commitment to provide a financially sound social security system that would take at least some of the worry out of the financial consequences of growing old. The original Social Security Act provided only for payments to retired employees age 65 or over who had made enough contributions to the fund to be covered under the system. Over the years Congress has amended the act and expanded coverage.

- In 1939, a change in the law added survivors' benefits and benefits for the retiree's spouse and children.
- Disability benefits were added in 1956.
- Medicare was added in 1965.

Eligibility for benefits has also been modified over the years.

- In 1956 the age at which women could first receive Social Security benefits was lowered from 65 to 62 with a reduction in benefits for those who chose the early retirement option.
- In 1961 men also became eligible to receive reduced benefits as early as age 62.

This trend of lowering age requirements was reversed with the 1983 amendments to the Social Security Act. Because projected long-term financial problems threatened Social Security solvency and, over time, people are living longer, the 1983 changes provided for a gradual increase in the retirement age from 65 to 66 by the year 2009 and to 67 by 2027.

The term "social security" was not in widespread use in 1935 at the time the Social Security Act was passed. The original title of the bill to create social security was the Economic Security Act. During the bill's consideration in Congress it was renamed the Social Security Act, which became the familiar term from that point forward. *The entire Social Security program is now referred to as OASDHI which stands for Old Age Survivors, Disability, and Health Insurance. Although we usually refer to The Social Security Trust Fund, there are actually three trust funds: the Old-Age and Survivors Insurance Trust Fund, the Disability Insurance Trust Fund, and the Federal Hospital Insurance Trust Fund.*

FROM 1937 UNTIL 1940, Social Security paid benefits in the form of a single, lump-sum payment in order to provide some "payback" to those people who contributed to the program but would not participate long enough to be vested for monthly benefits. Under the 1935 law, monthly benefits were to begin in 1942, with the period 1937-1942 used both to build up the trust fund and to provide a minimum period for people to participate in order to qualify for monthly benefits.

According to the Social Security Administration, the earliest reported applicant for a lump-sum benefit was a retired Cleveland motorman named Ernest Ackerman, who retired one day after the Social Security program began. During his one day of participation in the program, a nickel was withheld from Mr. Ackerman's pay for Social Security. In return, he received a lump-sum payment of 17 cents. The average lump-sum payment during this period was $58.06. A woman named Ida May Fuller, from Ludlow, Vermont, was the first recipient of monthly Social Security benefits.

Until recent decades, Americans have felt confident that their retirement benefits would be available when they needed them. They trusted their government to manage the funds they had contributed wisely and responsibly. President Roosevelt's determination that Social Security funds be kept separate from general revenue funds was crystal clear. Senator Moynihan spoke of Roosevelt's strong commitment on the floor of the Senate on October 9, 1990. The following excerpts from his speech are taken from the Congressional Record.

> We know one thing in particular: President Roosevelt was absolutely determined that the payments made into this system would be credited to the individual who had paid them. Each individual would have an account recording every nickel he and his employer put in, and a passbook in the form of a Social Security card with his or her name on it.
>   . . . In 1941, Luther Gulick, a very distinguished professor at Columbia University went in to see President Roosevelt. . . . Professor Gulick suggested that perhaps the time had come to stop levying pay-

roll taxes separately from income taxes. Gulick went back and wrote a memorandum of the conversation. The president replied. He said:

"I guess you are right on the economics, but those taxes were never a problem of economics. We put those payroll contributions in so as to give the contributors a legal, moral, and political right to collect their pension and unemployment benefits with those taxes in there. No damned politician can ever scrap my Social Security Program."

Roosevelt wanted a financially sound Social Security trust fund that the American people could have confidence in. Social Security was an insurance program and the fees paid into it were considered insurance payments. Roosevelt could not have imagined a time when politicians would treat these insurance contributions as the equivalent of general revenue taxes.

However, the events of the past two decades have led many Americans to question how committed their political leaders are to keeping the fund solvent for future generations. The Social Security program has become a resource for political maneuvering and a mask for irresponsible fiscal policies. Most of the abuse and misuse of the Social Security trust fund followed passage of legislation in 1983 that was supposed to raise—not lower—confidence in the long-term solvency of the program.

As reported in Chapter 1, the 1983 legislation was enacted to improve the solvency of the Social Security trust fund, which had run small budget deficits for seven years in a row from 1976-1982. Both Social Security tax rates and the Social Security tax base were gradually raised over a seven-year period so the trust fund would be solvent when it took the big financial hit around 2010.

Unfortunately, instead of using the increased Social Security revenue to build up the size of the trust fund for future retirees, as was intended, the government began using it to fund other government programs as soon as the surplus first appeared in 1983, and it has continued to do so ever since. This practice has been obscuring the true size of federal budget deficits because, since 1983, the government has been subtracting the surplus in the Social Security trust fund from the deficit in the operating budget, reporting an official budget deficit that has been billions of dollars below the actual figure.

Table 2 shows the actual size of the Social Security surplus for every year from 1983 to 2003, and the cumulative totals of Social Security dollars borrowed by the government and used for non-Social Security purposes for each year in the period. The seventh consecutive deficit was $7.9 billion in 1982, the last year before enactment of the 1983 tax increases.

Both 1983 and 1984 were essentially break-even years with only tiny surpluses. Since 1985, however, the revenue-generating capacity of the 1983 tax hikes has been obvious:

- The $9.4 billion Social Security surplus of 1985 increased tenfold by 1998, with a surplus of $99.2 billion recorded for that year.
- In 1996, just 13 years after the tax increase, the fund had accumulated surpluses of more than half a trillion dollars.
- By 2003 the cumulative surplus was approaching $1.5 trillion.

Every dollar of the $1.5 trillion cumulative surplus belonged to the Social Security trust fund and to the millions of individuals who had made contributions to it. Yet, as of late 2003, not a dollar of the $1.5 trillion was left in the fund.

The kindest thing we can say is that the government "borrowed" every penny in the fund and spent it on other things. But the word "borrowed" implies repayment. None of the funds have been repaid to date, and I don't expect to see very much, if any, of the money to ever be repaid, because that would require substantial tax increases.

The government leaders who currently hold office, both in the legislative and executive branches of government, are so politically motivated that I can't imagine them raising taxes—even to honor the commitment that the government has made to repay the borrowed

TABLE 2

SOCIAL SECURITY SURPLUS 1983–2003
(In Billions of Dollars)

Year	Social Security Surplus for the Year	Cumulative Social Security Surpluses, 1983 and After	Cumulative Social Security Funds Borrowed and Spent for Non-Social Security Purposes, 1983 and After
1983	+0.2	0.2	0.2
1984	+0.3	0.5	0.5
1985	+9.4	9.9	9.9
1986	+16.7	26.6	26.6
1987	+19.6	46.2	46.2
1988	+38.8	84.4	84.4
1989	+52.8	137.2	137.2
1990	+56.6	193.8	193.8
1991	+52.2	250.4	250.4
1992	+50.1	300.5	300.5
1993	+45.3	345.8	345.8
1994	+55.7	401.5	401.5
1995	+62.4	463.9	463.9
1996	+66.6	530.5	530.5
1997	+81.4	611.9	611.9
1998	+99.2	711.1	711.1
1999	+123.7	834.8	834.8
2000	+149.8	984.6	984.6
2001	+160.7	1145.3	1145.3
2002	+159.7	1305.0	1305.0
2003*	+163.5	1464.7	1464.7

Source: Economic Report of the President, 2003
*Estimate

funds. There are, of course, some exceptions among members of Congress, but not nearly enough to muster a majority vote. And President George W. Bush seems absolutely determined to use every dollar he can get his hands on to repay his political supporters with tax cuts.

If the money is never repaid, then we must use the word "stolen"—not "borrowed"—to describe what happened to the reserves from the Social Security trust fund. It is probably not much of an exaggeration to say that recent presidents and members of Congress have embezzled at least $1.5 trillion of the revenue generated by the 1983 Social Security tax increases, revenue that was specifically earmarked for funding the retirement of the largest generation in American history.

This practice of embezzlement was strongly challenged by Senator Daniel Patrick Moynihan in 1990 when he proposed cutting Social Security taxes. As pointed out in Chapter 1, Senator Moynihan had been a strong supporter of the 1983 efforts to strengthen the Social Security system. He had served on the commission that recommended the plan that involved gradually raising the Social Security tax rate from 6.7 percent in 1983 to 7.65 percent in 1990, and raising the tax base from $35,700 in 1983 to $51,300 in 1990.

Senator Moynihan was outraged that, instead of being used to build up the size of the Social Security trust fund for future retirees as was intended, the surplus in the Social Security fund was being used to pay for general government spending by investing it in Treasury Securities. Senator Moynihan, who felt the American people were being betrayed and deceived, proposed undoing the 1983 legislation by cutting Social Security taxes so there would be no surplus to mask the enormous deficits in the operating budget.

Senator Moynihan expressed his concern about the integrity of the Social Security fund in a speech on the Senate floor on October 9, 1990. The following are excerpts from that speech.

Mr. MOYNIHAN. Mr. President, I rise as chairman of the Subcommittee on Social Security to offer this freestanding bill which has been contemplated in the body for the whole of this second session of the

101st Congress and, indeed, prior to that in the setting of a series of studies and commissioned reports which have come to us on the fate of the Social Security trust funds.

The essence of the question, Mr. President, is that we now have a situation where the Social Security trust funds . . . are now running, and have for a number of years been running, a very large surplus, and they will continue to run such a surplus for the next 30 years.

. . . the fact . . . is that in an absolutely unprecedented pattern not known to any modern State of which I am aware and certainly never known to the Social Security System which is now in its second half century . . . the U.S. Government has begun to use a surplus in the fund as if it were general revenue.

This is not just a small stream of general revenue which could be thought of as incidental for maintenance of a large system. To the contrary, it is one of the primary sources of revenue of the Federal Government.

The trust funds are now rising at approximately $1.5 billion a week, and will shortly be rising at $2 billion, soon $3 billion, then $4 billion a week. They will, in sum, accumulate a surplus of some $3 trillion in the next 30 years. Three trillion dollars is a sizable sum. The stocks of all the companies listed on the New York Stock Exchange would sell for about $3 trillion.

This money is coming in. It is the largest revenue stream in the history of public finance. One of the extraordinary facts is that it has come upon us almost unawares, and we have yet to make a decision about how to treat these moneys. Today we can begin that decision process. It is, I would like to suggest, Mr. President, a fateful decision, because the integrity of our revenue system is at stake.

. . . . The point about these moneys, Mr. President, is that we refer to them as taxes, as payroll taxes, and yet they are not taxes. They are payments, payments into an insurance fund.

On the same day, Senator Reid of Nevada also had strong words of condemnation for the practice of using Social Security trust funds surpluses as general revenue.

Mr. REID. Mr. President . . . I would like to talk about the Social Security trust fund in a number of other difficult perspectives for a few minutes this morning. . . .

I practiced law before coming to the Senate. Like most attorneys who have an office practice where they deal with clients who have problems, I had a trust fund set up for my clients. If there were ever a time where money came into my office that was my client's money, that money had to go into a trust fund.

Mr. President, before that money was distributed out of that trust fund, we had to make sure that money went to the client. That money could not be used to make car payments for me, house payments for me, or buy a present for one of my children. That money could only be used for the purpose for which it was placed in that trust fund.

The same basic rule should apply to the Social Security trust fund. Those moneys should be used only for the purpose for which the money is collected. If, when I practiced law, I violated that trust, I could be subject to disbarment. I could be subject to administrative procedures being taken against me by the Bar Association. In fact, I could be criminally prosecuted by the district attorney.

That is what this discussion is all about. The discussion is are we as a country violating a trust by spending Social Security trust fund moneys for some purpose other than for which they were intended. The obvious answer is yes.

The president, who is a party in this violation of trust, along with members of Congress, is not being brought before a Bar Association for purposes of disbarment or some type of administrative remedy. There is no prosecuting authority saying, Mr. President, what you have done is illegal. But the fact is it is wrong; what has taken place is wrong. . . .

. . . I think that is a very good illustration of what I was talking about, embezzlement, thievery. Because that, Mr. President, is what we are talking about here. But for the dialog started by the Senator from New York, we would not be here today. And I publicly commend and applaud the vigorous activity generated by the Senator from New York because on that chart in emblazoned red letters is what has been tak-

ing place here, embezzlement. During the period of growth we have
had during the past 10 years, the growth has been from two sources.
One, a large credit card with no limits on it, and, two, we have been
stealing money from the Social Security recipients of this country. . . .
Maybe what we should do in conjunction with the president, to
really carry this conspiracy to its appropriate end, is rather than having it called the Social Security trust fund, why do we not change it and
call it the "Social Security slush fund?"

Using Social Security revenue to pay for non-Social Security programs was more than wrong. It was illegal! At least it became illegal
on November 5, 1990, when President Bush signed into law the Budget Enforcement Act of 1990. Section 13301 of this law specifically
mandated that Social Security trust fund money be kept separate from
general revenue funds.

Senator Hollings, who had pushed for the new law, had hoped that
by making it illegal for the Congress and the president to include
Social Security funds in their budget calculations the deliberate
deception of the public would come to an end. But nothing changed.
The Bush administration and many members of Congress deliberately
and knowingly violated the new federal law and continued to embezzle the surplus Social Security funds.

One of the reasons that it has been so easy for the past three presidents to deceive the American people about the true financial condition of the United States Government is the fact that any Social
Security surplus funds are by law supposed to be invested in U.S. Treasury securities. Under current law, the Social Security funds cannot be
invested in stocks or bonds, only Treasury securities. But this does not
in any way necessitate or justify the using of surplus funds to finance
general government operations. Every dollar of Social Security revenue in excess of what is required to pay current benefits should be
used to pay down the gigantic national debt, thereby putting the
money into a separate "bank account" that was off limits to politicians
who were tempted to borrow the funds to pay for general government

operations. *The fiscally responsible thing to do between now and 2018 is to use Social Security funds to pay down the national debt during the Social Security surplus years, then borrow those dollars back during the deficit years that will come after 2018. The surplus monies would be invested in government securities as required by law, but they would not be available for funding general government programs.*

No president prior to Ronald Reagan had access to significant surplus Social Security revenue, so there was no temptation to violate the spirit of the law that requires Social Security funds to be kept separate from general government revenue. However, during the second term of the Reagan administration, $84.5 billion in Social Security surplus funds became available, and these funds were used to fund general government operations and mask the true size of the federal deficit.

Reagan's successor, George Bush, had even more Social Security surplus money available to divert into the coffers of general government revenue, and he diverted the entire $211.7 billion. Although President Clinton did reduce the huge budget deficits by raising income taxes, cutting spending, and promoting a prosperous economy that resulted in eliminating the on-budget deficit in 1999, he also participated in the charade that portrayed government finances as being much better than they actually were. And Clinton, too, used Social Security surpluses for general government financing.

George W. Bush wins the prize, though, for posing the greatest threat to Social Security. He pushed through Congress two large tax cuts that led to massive new budget deficits. Bush used Social Security tax dollars, paid by working Americans, to help fund the tax cuts that went mostly to the wealthiest Americans.

Table 3 shows how the surplus in the Social Security trust fund served to conceal the true size of the deficit in the government's operating budget. As you can see, the Social Security (off-budget) surplus was nonexistent until 1983 and, for all practical purposes, was insignificant until 1985 when it reached the $9.4 billion level as the increased Social Security tax dollars flowed into the trust fund. Five years later, in 1990, the surplus had soared to $56.6 billion. That is when the political fireworks began. There was a $277.8 billion deficit in the government's operating budget that year, and every penny of the Social Security surplus was used to help finance the huge on-budget (operating) deficit.

The Budget Enforcement Act of 1990 made substantial changes in the budget process. Among them was the removal of the income and outgo of the Social Security trust funds from all calculations of the federal budget, including the budget deficit or surplus. This exclusion applied to the budget prepared by the president, the federal budgets formulated by the Congress, and the budget process provisions designed to reduce and control the budget deficits.

In 1969, a time when Congress did not have a budget-making process, President Lyndon Johnson administratively began officially counting Social Security funds as part of the Federal Budget. Increased spending for programs initiated or expanded during the "Great Society" era, combined with escalating military expenditures on the Vietnam war, heightened concern in Congress about budget deficits and spending controls. In response to the perceived encroachment of the executive branch on the budgetary turf of the legislative branch of government, Congress passed the Congressional Budget and Impoundment Control Act of 1974. The major purposes of this act were to reassert the congressional role in budgeting, to add some centralizing influence to the federal budget process, and to constrain the use of presidential impoundments (refusal to spend) of appropriated funds. In addition, The House and Senate Budget Committees were created to coordinate the congressional consideration of the budget, and the Congressional Budget Office was established as a source of nonpartisan analysis and information relating to the budget and the economy. With passage of the Congressional Budget and Impoundment Control Act, Congress adopted a process for developing budget goals, and these goals also officially counted Social Security as part of the "unified budget."

These actions did not sit well with the public, and Senator Moynihan's efforts to make the public aware of just how the Social Security

TABLE 3

ON-BUDGET AND OFF-BUDGET SURPLUSES OR DEFICITS, 1976–2003

(In Billions of Dollars)

Year	On-budget Surplus (+) or Deficit (-)	Off-budget Surplus (+) or Deficit (-)	Official Surplus (+) or Deficit (-) Reported (*Based on Unified Budget*)	Actual Surplus (+) or Deficit (-) (*Excluding Social Security*)
1976	-70.5	-3.2	-73.7	-70.5
1977	-49.8	-3.9	-53.7	-49.8
1978	-54.9	-4.3	-59.2	-54.9
1979	-38.7	-2.0	-40.7	-38.7
1980	-72.7	-1.1	-73.8	-72.7
1981	-74.0	-5.0	-79.0	-74.0
1982	-120.1	-7.9	-128.0	-120.1
1983	-208.0	+0.2	-207.8	-208.0
1984	-185.7	+0.3	-185.4	-185.7
1985	-221.7	+9.4	-212.3	-221.7
1986	-238.0	+16.7	-221.3	-238.0
1987	-169.3	+19.6	-149.7	-169.3
1988	-194.0	+38.8	-155.2	-194.0
1989	-205.2	+52.8	-152.4	-205.2
1990	-277.8	+56.6	-221.2	-277.8
1991	-321.6	+52.2	-269.4	-321.6
1992	-340.5	+50.1	-290.4	-340.5
1993	-300.5	+45.3	-255.2	-300.5
1994	-258.9	+55.7	-203.2	-258.9
1995	-226.4	+62.4	-164.0	-226.4
1996	-174.1	+66.6	-107.5	-174.1
1997	-103.4	+81.4	-22.0	-103.4
1998	-30.0	+99.2	+69.2	-30.0
1999	+1.9	+123.7	+125.6	+1.9
2000	+86.6	+149.8	+236.4	+86.6
2001	-33.4	+160.7	+127.3	-33.4
2002	-317.5	+159.7	-157.8	-317.5
2003*	-467.6	+163.5	-304.1	-467.6

Source: Economic Report of the President, 2003
*Estimate

money was being used led to congressional concerns that the public's confidence in the program was being eroded. Increased public awareness also led to proposals to legally remove Social Security from the budget. Finally, in 1990, Congress reacted to the criticism that surplus Social Security taxes were masking the size of the budget deficits. It legally removed Social Security from the budget calculations.

In fiscal year 2002, the federal government collected $159.7 billion more in Social Security taxes than it paid out in Social Security benefits. What happened to the huge surplus? The same thing that happens to all surplus Social Security taxes—the money was used to pay for other government programs.

By law, Social Security trust fund surpluses are supposed to be invested in U.S. Treasury securities, which are supposed to be the safest of all investments, and interest is paid to the holders of Treasury securities. The only catch is that the government pays interest on funds borrowed from the Social Security trust fund by posting "special-issue" securities just like the ones it posted when it borrowed the money. *This means that both the assets and the earnings of the Social Security trust fund are in the form of government IOUs that have no commercial value.*

According to the 2003 Social Security Trustees Report:

- The Social Security surpluses that we have come to rely on will cease to exist by 2018, and the fund will run deficits thereafter.
- By the year 2042, it is expected that the system will be broke, and that year's Social Security revenue will be only enough to pay 73 percent of the benefits due that year.
- Each year thereafter, the gap between revenue and benefits due will become larger and larger, until inevitably it will be necessary either to raise taxes or substantially cut Social Security benefits.

As dismal as they are, these projections by the Social Security Trustees greatly understate the problems. They are based on the assumption that the federal government will repay the massive amounts it has borrowed from the Social Security fund when they are needed. Given the politics of the situation, this is not likely to happen. The trust funds do not represent a pool of cash savings that can be drawn down to make benefit payments. They are simply bookkeeping devices, and the special-issue U.S. Treasury bonds they contain represent nothing more than a promise from one arm of the government (Treasury) to pay off IOUs held by another arm of government (Social Security).

According to "Lessons From The 2003 Social Security Trustees Report," released May 20, 2003, by the Concord Coalition, a nonpartisan organization dedicated to sound budget policy and a solvent Social Security system,

> What matters in the real world is not some official "solvency" measure but Social Security's operating balance—that is, the annual difference between cash in and cash out. According to the Trustees' report, by 2018 Social Security's cash in will no longer exceed the cash out. At that point, the trust fund bonds will need to be converted into cash to pay promised benefits. To do so, Congress will need to cut spending for other programs, borrow from the public, or raise taxes, or some combination of all three.

Long-term deficits in the Social Security system far outweigh near-term surpluses. Although, because of the 1983 tax increases, Social Security is generating annual surpluses now, large and growing deficits loom in the not-too-distant future. Social Security is projected to generate a $1.1 trillion cash surplus between now and 2018, but from 2018 through 2077 (the end of the Social Security Trustees' evaluation period) Social Security is expected to run a *cumulative cash deficit of $26 trillion*, primarily because of the retirement of the baby boomers.

Something must be done to reform the system in the near future. Failure to act, according to the Social Security Trustees, would result in a 26 percent cut in benefits by 2042, or a 34 percent increase in taxes. Borrowing the money to pay benefits would add approximately $7 trillion to the national debt by 2042, and $52 trillion by 2077, including interest. We must not leave such a legacy to our children and grandchildren.

It is difficult to motivate lawmakers to take action in the short run to resolve long-term problems. But the Social Security problem is at the crisis stage right now. The robbery is currently underway so there is still time to nab the robbers. The planned surpluses designed to build up a reserve are being embezzled on a daily basis. These temporary, planned surpluses are why there is more cash inflow into the system than there is cash outflow in the form of benefits. As long as annual revenue exceeds annual benefit payments, the long-term problem is not obvious. However, the annual surpluses will be transformed into annual deficits beginning in 2018. From that time forward, there will not be enough current income to pay current benefits. That is when the Social Security program will need the reserve money that is supposed to be in the trust fund.

The problem is that there is no money in the trust fund. Every dollar of past Social Security surpluses has been "borrowed" and spent for other things by the federal government. The only thing in the trust fund is "special-issue," nonmarketable government IOUs. You can't pay benefits with these IOUs, and you can't sell them. For all practical purposes, they are worthless unless the government is willing to raise taxes or find some other way to repay the massive amounts of money it has "borrowed" from the Social Security fund over the past 20 years. Government officials argue that the IOUs in the trust fund are far from worthless because they are backed up by the "full faith and credit of the United States government." But just how much faith can we have in a government that has deceived the public about the status of federal finances for two decades?

Now is the time to stop the thievery. Now is the time to demand that the government keep its sticky fingers off the Social Security money. The fact that not all of the Social Security money currently coming in is needed to pay benefits today is no excuse to misappropriate the funds. Unless the government has a specific, foolproof plan for repaying people's Social Security money when they need it, the government should not touch a dollar of it. Otherwise, not only will there no longer be a Social Security surplus for the government to borrow, but the government's obligation to retirees to pay benefits due will exceed the revenue coming in from the payroll tax. Given the fact that the U.S. Government has been unable to balance its budget for the past 30 years, except in 1999 and 2000—even in years when it was able to borrow Social Security surplus funds—how in the world will it manage to balance the budget in the future and also pay back borrowed funds? That is a question all Americans should ask both themselves and those politicians who are behaving as if the nation had more money than it knows what to do with.

Starting in about 2010, Social Security benefit payments will begin to soar, and by 2018, the Social Security fund will begin running growing annual deficits. The interest earnings from past surpluses will keep the fund afloat for a while, if the government actually pays the interest instead of just issuing more IOUs, but just a few years farther down the road, it will be necessary for the government to start repaying the principal it owes the Social Security trust fund in order for the fund to remain solvent.

If the government does not fully repay its obligations to the Social Security trust fund, with interest, whenever the funds are needed, benefits would have to be reduced. Furthermore, the Social Security fund would not be actuarially sound on a long-term basis, even if the government were to repay all it owes with interest. I find it far more likely that the government will cut Social Security benefits than that it will raise taxes in order to repay its debt to the Social Security trust fund.

Finally, in 2042, even if the government has repaid every penny it owes the Social Security system, along with interest, the fund will no longer *be able* to pay full benefits. At that time, it is estimated that the Social Security System will be receiving only enough revenue to cover 73 percent of its annual obligations, and it will have no reserves to fall back on.

CHAPTER THREE

Economic Illiteracy
and Malpractice

~

Beware of the majority when mentally poisoned with misinforma-
tion, for collective ignorance does not become wisdom.

—William J. H. Boetcker, Presbyterian minister, 1873-1962

$\mathscr{A}$ BRAHAM LINCOLN ONCE SAID, "You can fool all of
the people some of the time, and you can fool some of the
people all of the time, but you can't fool all of the people all of the
time." I think it depends partly on whether or not the people want to
be fooled. In the area of government finance, it seems that for the past
23 years most of the people have been fooled most of the time by four
different presidents.

None of us would entrust our individual health to an accountant,
or a lawyer, no matter how brilliant the individual might be. Nor
would any of us entrust the maintenance and repair of our automobile to anyone but a highly skilled and well-trained auto technician.
If we are so particular about who does the maintenance and repair of
our automobile, why would we not insist that the maintenance and
repair of that far-more-complex mechanism called the American
economy also be performed under the guidance, at least, of highly
trained experts?

In the early 1980s, even before the Reagan administration had implemented any of its voodoo economics, Americans were warned of the dangers inherent in Reagan's proposals. The man who rang the warning bell was Paul Samuelson, not just a highly trained expert, but one of the most brilliant economists who ever lived, and the first American to receive the coveted Nobel prize in economics. Samuelson, who wrote a regular column for *Newsweek* at the time, had access to a mass audience, and he did everything in his power to alert his readers to the potentially disastrous consequences of Reagan's economic proposals. Below is an excerpt from an article by Samuelson that appeared in the March 2, 1981 issue of *Newsweek*.

> Reagan's program does attempt a radical break with the past. A radical-right crusade is being sold as a solution for an economy allegedly in crisis. There is no such crisis! Our people should join this crusade only if they agree with its philosophical conservative merits. They should not be flim-flammed by implausible promises that programs to restore the 1920s' inequalities will cure the inflation problem.

Dr. Samuelson tried his heart out to alert America to the dangers it was facing. But it was to no avail. His warnings fell mostly on deaf ears. Very few Americans cared about what professional economists thought, even Nobel prize-winning economists. They believed whatever the charismatic Reagan told them. He had promised that he could deliver a major tax cut and still balance the budget by 1984. Why should people take Samuelson's word over that of a president who had just been elected by a landslide? Never mind that Reagan chose a 34-year-old with no training in economics as the chief architect of his economic policy or that he ignored the advice of his own Council of Economic Advisers. Surely the President knew what he was doing.

Although Reagan's policies inflicted great damage on the American economy and the fiscal status of the federal government, he continued to insist, throughout his presidency, that "The American economy has never been healthier or stronger." Reaganomics had led to catastrophic deficits and a skyrocketing national debt, but instead of acknowledging the fact and taking remedial actions, Reagan just kept reiterating that his economic policies were sound. And the most disturbing part of it all is that, despite the abundant evidence to the contrary, the American people continued to believe him.

What had worked for the "great communicator" did not, however, work for his successor. When George Bush tried to follow in Reagan's footsteps, he was unable to convince Americans, who knew otherwise, that the economy was sound. Although President Bush seemed such a sure bet for reelection in 1992 that most of the top contenders for the Democratic nomination chose not to run, Bill Clinton wisely saw the incumbent president as vulnerable because of the state of the economy and the negative effects of Reaganomics.

Ronald Reagan was guilty of extreme economic malpractice, and his irresponsible policies cost the nation dearly. Even today, American taxpayers are paying approximately $500 million in interest, each and every day, on the $3 trillion added to the national debt just during the Reagan-Bush administrations. Economic malpractice occurs when policy makers pursue economic practices and policies that are not consistent with sound economic principles, as viewed by the majority of professionally trained economists, and when such unsound practices inflict damage on the economy.

In the medical field, when doctors take actions inconsistent with what the majority of doctors consider to be sound medicine, and such actions result in injury to the patient, the patient is entitled to sue the doctor for damages resulting from malpractice. Doctors are not entitled to experiment with their patients. They must stick to medical treatments that have proved effective in the past and are generally supported by the majority of medical professionals. Doctors who deliberately deviate from these standards may lose their medical license to practice and may be ordered by the courts to pay millions of dollars in damages.

Yet during the early years of the Reagan administration the equivalent of radical experimental surgery was performed on the American

TABLE 4

INTEREST ON THE NATIONAL DEBT

Like everybody else, the federal government must pay interest on money that it borrows. The amount of the interest paid each year depends on the size of the debt and the current interest rate.

At the beginning of the twenty-first century, interest rates were the lowest they had been in more than 40 years. However, interest rates will not remain low indefinitely. When interest rates begin to rise, the government will have to pay more interest even if the size of the debt could somehow be held constant. If interest rates were to double, for example, the amount of interest paid each year would also double. And, of course, the higher the debt, the higher the amount of interest paid, even if the interest rate does not change.

The figures below show the size of the debt and the interest cost for 2000, 2001, and 2002. Note that although the debt grew larger each year, the total interest cost came down because of the historically low market interest rates.

Year	National Debt ($billions)	Interest Paid ($billions)
2002	6,198.4	332.54
2001	5,770.3	359.51
2000	5,629.0	362.00

Source: U.S. Treasury Department

Note that, in 2000, the total interest cost was almost $365 billion. That means that *American taxpayers paid approximately $1 billion per day in interest on the national debt during 2000.*

economy by government officials who had little knowledge of economics. Despite the fact that the majority of professionally trained economists did not support them, and over the protests of Nobel-prize-winning economists, these government officials implemented plans that adversely affected millions of people.

When a medical doctor steps outside the bounds of traditional and conventional medicine (by endorsing and supporting doctor-assisted suicide, for example), it becomes a worldwide news story. This results in widespread public debate that sometimes leads to definitive curbs on nontraditional practices. However, when government policy makers take actions that are detrimental to the long-term health of the economy in order to practice what appears to be good short-term politics, rarely is the public made aware of them by the news media.

It's not that journalists have no interest in reporting economic malpractice. The problem is that most journalists have had little or no formal instruction in economics, and would not be able to recognize economic malpractice. It is not their fault or the fault of the majority of Americans in most fields, who also lack education in the field of economics. It is the fault of the American educational system.

Widespread economic illiteracy poses one of the greatest threats to America's future, and it is the primary cause of all past economic malpractice. Economic illiteracy threatens our future, both as individuals and as a nation. This major national problem is evidenced by the following excerpt from the June 14, 1999, issue of *U.S. News & World Report.*

> On a recent nationwide test of basic economic principles, two thirds of the 1,085 high school students who took it did not even know that the stock market is where people buy and sell shares—never mind that investments can tumble. Worse, few understood that scarcity drives up prices or that money loses value in times of inflation—two consumer fundamentals. Average grade: F

The magazine article refers to a study conducted by Louis Harris

& Associates on behalf of the National Council on Economic Education. The survey is based on interviews with a national cross section of 1,010 adults aged 18 and over and a representative sample of 1,085 students in grades 9 through 12.

The results of the survey are shocking. On average, adults got a grade of 57 percent for their knowledge of basic economics compared to an average score of only 48 percent for high school students. Specifically, only 37 percent of adults and 36 percent of students recognized that the statement, "money holds its value well in times of inflation" is incorrect. In the area of public finance, only 54 percent of adults and 23 percent of high school students knew that when the federal government spends more in a year than it collects in revenue for that year, there is a budget deficit. Also, 22 percent of adults and 25 percent of students confuse the definition of a budget deficit with the national debt.

The National Council on Economic Education, which commissioned the national survey of economic literacy, is a nonprofit partnership of leaders in education, business, and labor. The council has established a nationwide network of state councils and over 260 university-based centers to train teachers to teach economics to our nation's young people. One week after releasing the shocking results of its national survey on economic literacy, the Council announced an ambitious five-year, nationwide campaign to increase economic literacy among both students and adults.

Although economics has a greater impact on our daily lives than almost any other academic subject, most high school graduates are never exposed to the subject. In addition, most college graduates have not taken a single course in economics. All high school students are required to study American history and American government, presumably so they will be "better citizens" and "better-informed" voters. This is good, but it is impossible to have a clear understanding of either United States history or American government without a clear understanding of basic economic principles and a knowledge of how the American economy operates.

Economic illiteracy is one of America's greatest threats. It has played a leading role in economic malpractice in the past, and it is the primary reason that most Americans believed the hoax that the nation had a huge budget surplus, as many top politicians were claiming as recently as 2002.

Most members of Congress and other top government officials would probably fail a general test on economic literacy. Most have never had a course in economics, but still think they know enough about the subject to pass judgment on which economic proposals are sound and which are not. Add to their number the many journalists who are economically illiterate, and it is easy to see how economic malpractice became rampant. *The public is not informed enough to be concerned.* This has gotten the nation into great trouble in the past and will continue to do so in the future.

The primary problem is that many people, including members of Congress and other top government officials, know very little about economics but think they know a great deal. They have an extremely simplistic notion of what economics is about and believe that they are capable of making decisions about it without consulting experts. Many have the mistaken notion that economics is a business subject. It is not. It is a highly complex social science.

Economics can be defined as *the study of how individuals and society choose to use limited resources in an effort to satisfy people's unlimited wants.* But there is so much more to it than this simplified definition suggests. There are some elements of common sense in the study of economics but, overall, economics is a highly sophisticated science. The following short excerpt from the article on economics in *Encyclopedia Americana* is a good summary of the scientific nature of the field of economics.

> Like medicine or engineering, economics is a rigorous discipline. Hard thinking has produced hypotheses, and those hypotheses have been tested by empirical observation and, where possible, by careful measurement. When the results turned out to be inconsistent with the hypotheses, more hard thinking came up with new hypotheses. The

method of economics, then, is not different from the methods of other sciences.

Economics is one of the six categories in which the coveted Nobel prize is awarded to persons "who have made outstanding contributions for the benefit of mankind." The other five categories are, medicine, physics, chemistry, literature, and peace.

Congress would never consider enacting legislation on medicine, physics, or chemistry, without considering the views of experts in these fields. Yet, during the Reagan administration, Budget Director David Stockman, who had never had even an introductory course in the field of economics, became the chief architect of economic policy and totally ignored and defied the warnings of outstanding professional economists, some of whom had been awarded the Nobel Prize.

America is paying an enormous price for economic malpractice. Yet, in the 2000 presidential election, the American people elected a new president who was advocating proposals, including a major tax cut, that are totally contrary to the thinking of most mainstream professional economists. Most Americans, including top government officials, do not know much more about economics than they know about chemistry or physics. However, they are aware that they don't know much about chemistry or physics, but unaware that they are equally illiterate in the field of economics.

Absolutely everything the government does affects the economy in some way, either positively or negatively. So even when it takes certain actions that have no intended impact on the economy, we can be sure that the actions will affect it in some way. In the field of medicine, doctors know that treating a patient for one medical problem can make another problem even worse. Extensive research has been done to determine potential side effects of any potential given course of treatment, and doctors exercise great caution in an effort to avoid harming the patient in some other way when they treat him or her for any particular condition.

Because there are many unintentional economic side effects to all major government actions a careful analysis of any proposed action should be made by competent, professionally trained economists before the action is taken, and the findings of the economists should be taken into consideration by policy makers.

It is especially critical to note that any increase or decrease in government spending and any increase or decrease in taxes will have a significant impact on the performance of the economy. The nature of this impact will depend on the stage of the business cycle in which the economy is currently operating. If the economy is in a severe recession with high unemployment, either a specifically targeted increase in government spending or a properly structured temporary decrease in taxes can have a positive effect.

The additional purchase of goods and services resulting from a direct increase in government spending, and the increased consumer spending resulting from the additional "take-home" pay following a tax cut, will increase total spending (aggregate demand) and thereby help the economy to recover from the recession. Thus, in times of recession and high unemployment, any actions that result in an increase in aggregate demand will have a positive impact on the performance of the economy. However, at a time when the economy is at the peak of the business cycle, with very low unemployment and labor shortages, an increase in government spending or a decrease in taxes is just about the worst thing the government could do.

Regardless of the state of the economy, it is crucial that short-term efforts to stimulate the economy with tax cuts be temporary, and targeted at consumer spending. Permanent cuts in taxes can wreak havoc with the budget in the long term and result in massive future deficits and soaring growth in the national debt.

Probably the first time that any administration was guilty of economic malpractice was during the Great Depression. However, it is hard to hold Hoover responsible because modern economic science was still in its infancy. And, although Roosevelt was slow to take the correct actions, he did gradually implement fairly sound economic policies.

During the late 1920s, the economy was strong and prosperous.

However, during the Great Depression of the 1930s, the nation experienced enormous poverty and suffering. The unemployment rate reached 25 percent, and millions of Americans were hungry and homeless. Yet, at a time when men, women, and children picked through garbage in search of food, sheep raisers in the western states slaughtered sheep by the thousands and destroyed their carcasses. The market price for sheep had fallen below the cost of shipping them to market, so that farmers would lose money if they did so. And while millions of Americans were without bread, wheat was left in the fields uncut because the price of wheat was too low to cover the harvesting costs.

In addition, many of the nation's factories, that could have been turning out goods and providing the jobs that Americans wanted and needed so desperately, sat partially or totally idle. The factories did not operate because they couldn't sell their products, and people couldn't buy the products because they didn't have jobs. The American economic system was simply allowed to break down, and it remained broken down for a decade.

The cost of the Great Depression was astronomical. According to estimates by economic historians, if the economy had fully used all of its resources during the 1930s, the dollar value of the additional production would have been higher than the cost of World War II. This would have been enough money to have covered the cost of a new house, and several new cars, for every American family during that decade.

The real tragedy is that the Great Depression never really needed to happen. The nation had all the productive resources necessary to produce a prosperous lifestyle during the 1930s just as it did in the 1920s. However, many of the resources were allowed to remain idle while millions were hungry and homeless. The policy makers of the 1930s can, however, be excused to some degree for letting that happen, because modern economics was still young and untested.

After Franklin Roosevelt was first elected president, he continued to follow many of the same economic policies that Hoover had followed. However, he gradually began to adopt some of the principles of modern economics that had been introduced by British economist,

John Maynard Keynes. In 1936, Keynes published a monumental book called, *The General Theory of Employment, Interest, and Money.* In it, Keynes set forth a new economic theory that became known as Keynesian economics.

Keynesian economics soon became the predominant body of economic theory in the Western world. Keynes came to the United States and met with President Roosevelt in an effort to persuade him to use the new economic knowledge to bring the economy out of the depression. After Professor Keynes left, Roosevelt reportedly told an aide that he hadn't understood what Keynes had said.

The *New York Times* requested that Keynes spell out his view on the American outlook in an article for publication. Given the desperate conditions of the Great Depression, Americans were hungry for any new ideas or signs of hope that might lead the nation back toward prosperity. In response to the request, Keynes chose to write "An Open Letter to President Roosevelt" which he sent to the *Times.*

The letter, which appeared in the *New York Times* on December 31, 1936, and was syndicated in other parts of the United States, was long and detailed. The first and last of the 19 points Keynes addressed in his letter to President Roosevelt are reproduced below to give the reader some feel for the tone of the letter.

Dear Mr. President,

1. You have made yourself the Trustee for those in every country who seek to mend the evils of our condition by reasoned experiment within the framework of the existing social system. If you fail, rational change will be gravely prejudiced throughout the world, leaving orthodoxy and revolution to fight it out. But if you succeed, new and bolder methods will be tried everywhere, and we may date the first chapter of a new economic era from your accession to office. This is a sufficient reason why I should venture to lay my reflections before you, though under the disadvantages of distance and partial knowledge . . .

19. With these adaptations or enlargements of your existing policies, I should expect a successful outcome with great confidence. How much

that would mean, not only to the material prosperity of the United States and the whole World, but in comfort to men's minds through a restoration of their faith in the wisdom and the power of Government!

> With great respect,
> Your obedient servant
> J. M. Keynes

Roosevelt gradually became a convert to the new economic thinking and began pursuing policies, including public-employment programs, that would stimulate aggregate demand and put the unemployed back to work. The economy did improve, but Roosevelt and the Congress were not willing to provide a strong enough dose of medicine to truly get the economy back on track. It was the massive spending on World War II that returned it to prosperity.

It is extremely important to note that *it was not the war itself, but the spending on the war* that provided sufficient aggregate demand to return the economy to full employment. If there had never been a war, but the government had spent as much as it did on the war on other projects such as building roads, schools, hospitals, and so forth, the economy could have shown the same healthy economic growth that it did as a result of spending on the war.

As the war came to an end, there was much fear that without the war expenditures the economy would slip right back into a depression. In an effort to do everything possible to keep this from happening, Congress passed the Employment Act of 1946. This act pledged the commitment of the United States government to provide "conditions under which there will be afforded useful employment opportunities, including self-employment, for those able, willing, and seeking to work, and to promote maximum employment, production, and purchasing power."

As part of the Act, Congress set up a Council of Economic Advisers to the president, and required the president to send an annual economic report to the Congress, describing the state of the economy and suggesting improvements. Under this legislation, the president is mandated to select a Council of Economic Advisers so that he will always have access to trained professional economists who, theoretically, would guide him away from potential economic malpractice.

The problem is that some past presidents have totally ignored the advice of their own economic advisers and deliberately engaged in economic malpractice. President Lyndon B. Johnson was the first president to flagrantly violate the intent of the Employment Act of 1946 by turning his back on the sound economic advice of his economic advisers and listening instead to his political advisers.

President Johnson's economic advisers urged him to raise taxes to offset the substantial increase in military expenditures on the Vietnam War. They warned that failure to do so could set off a prolonged period of high inflation. However, Johnson's political advisers told him that to do so would not be good politics. They suggested that to tell the American people that they were going to have to pay more taxes because of the war would be the equivalent of political suicide. At that time, the war was becoming increasingly unpopular with the people, so they would be especially irritated at the prospects of paying higher taxes because of it. Johnson believed that raising taxes would prevent him from being elected to another term, and so he placed personal political considerations above pursuing sound economic policies. Later, when political polls indicated that Johnson was not likely to get reelected under any circumstances, he announced that he had decided not to seek reelection. It was at that time that Johnson called on Congress to enact a small temporary tax increase to head off inflation. A temporary 10 percent surtax was finally enacted in 1968 but it was more than two years too late to nip the inflationary pressures in the bud.

America paid an exhorbitant price for President Johnson's failure to listen to the advice of his own handpicked Council of Economic Advisers. In 1965, the economy was in one of the best positions ever. The unemployment rate was 4.5 percent, the inflation rate was 1.6 percent, and the government ran a budget deficit of only $1.4 billion.

This was the seventh year in a row that the inflation rate had remained below 2 percent, and the unemployment rate was at its lowest level in 8 years. The federal budget was almost in balance, and the nation exported more goods than it imported. And then we blew it!

The first major economic policy error was the failure of the government to curb the excess demand for goods and services during the late sixties. The escalation of the Vietnam War in 1966 led to a substantial unplanned increase in military expenditures. The large increase in government spending caused total spending to rise above the full-employment capacity of the economy. With total spending exceeding the capacity of the economy to produce, prices began to rise and the nation embarked on a long journey of demand-pull inflation.

Although it is easy to blame the Vietnam War for the inflation, it was not the war but the financing of the war that caused the inflationary problems. When military spending escalated in 1966, the economy was operating at the lowest level of unemployment—3.8 percent—in 13 years. Not since 1953 had the unemployment rate dropped below 4 percent. Thus, the economy was operating near its maximum capacity output, and any increase in any component of total spending would have to be offset by an equal decrease elsewhere, or demand-pull inflation would occur. If the government demanded an increase in the production of military goods, there would have to be a corresponding decrease in the production of domestic goods. And if rising prices were to be averted, any decrease in the production of consumer goods would have to be matched by an equal decrease in consumer spending.

This is why President Johnson's economic advisers argued for a tax increase to finance the increased military spending. Not only would the tax increase help to avoid deficits in the federal budget at a time of full employment, they argued, it would also reduce the disposable income of consumers and curtail their level of spending. A tax increase was just what the economy needed to avoid major inflation, but President Johnson was still very reluctant to call for a tax increase to finance an increasingly unpopular war.

When the president was finally convinced that a tax increase was absolutely necessary, Congress began to drag its feet. After a delay of more than two years, the much-needed increase was passed. But, by the time it was finally implemented, inflation was too far out of control to be stopped by a small tax increase. During the three years, 1966, 1967, and 1968, the federal government ran deficits totaling $37.7 billion. The economy was operating at full capacity, and therefore was not capable of any significant increase in the production of goods and services. Yet, during this three-year period, the government pumped $37.7 billion more into the economy in the form of spending than it took out in the form of taxes. This huge increase in purchasing power, which could not be matched by a similar increase in the supply of goods and services, could only lead to rising prices.

After seven years with inflation rates below 2 percent, the inflation rate rose to 2.9 percent in 1966, 4.2 percent in 1968, and 5.5 percent in 1969. The inflation was to get much worse during the 1970s and 1980s—11.0 percent in 1974, and 13.5 percent in 1980. Although much of the inflation of the 1970s resulted from the energy crises and soaring prices for crude oil, these special problems just added to the inflationary pressures started in the 1960s, when the government failed to raise taxes in time to prevent the increased spending on the Vietnam War from setting off a prolonged period of demand-pull inflation.

Although the name had not yet been invented, President Lyndon B. Johnson was clearly the first president to engage in large-scale voodoo economics. It took 16 years and the most severe economic downturn since the Great Depression (the 1981-82 recession) to break the back of the inflationary pressures set off by the economic malpractice of the Johnson years.

During the 1980 election campaign, candidate Ronald Reagan made one of the most irresistible promises ever made by any candidate for the presidency. He promised that if he were elected President, he would cut personal income tax rates by 30 percent over a three-year period.

"If I am elected president, I will cut personal income tax rates by 10 percent during my first year in office," Reagan promised a large crowd of enthusiastic supporters. As the applause began to build, Reagan raised his hand to quiet his admirers for a moment.

"Wait a minute," Mr. Reagan said. "I'm not done. I will cut your tax rates another 10 percent during my second year in office." This time Reagan allowed the cheers and applause to rise much higher before cutting them off.

"I have an encore," the candidate said as soon as the crowd was again quiet. "I will cut your tax rates an additional 10 percent during my third year for a total of 30 percent during my first three years as president!"

This time the crowd was allowed to cheer for as long as they wished. The "great communicator," with a lifetime of training and experience as a professional performer, was a master when it came to managing a crowd of enthusiastic supporters. And his message was sweeter than honey.

This performance was repeated again and again to crowds of enthusiastic supporters throughout the nation. And the good news didn't end with the promise of a 30 percent cut in tax rates. Candidate Reagan promised the crowds that he would simultaneously reduce both inflation and unemployment, avoid any major cuts in basic government services, build up the nation's military power, and "balance the federal budget by 1984."

Economists, including some recipients of the Nobel Prize, warned that Mr. Reagan could not deliver on these promises. And, during the Republican primary campaign, rival candidate George Bush referred to the economic package proposed by Reagan as "voodoo economics" which could lead to disaster if implemented. (This is believed to be the origin of the term, "voodoo economics," which has been widely used ever since.) But millions of Americans found the Reagan promises so attractive that they elected him president in a massive landslide victory over incumbent President Jimmy Carter.

On February 18, 1981, President Ronald Reagan delivered to a cheering joint session of Congress and a prime-time television audience a speech that marked a sharp turning point in American history. His "Program for Economic Recovery" represented a radical departure from the political and economic thinking that had dominated the American government for the past 40 years.

Among other things, President Reagan called for passage of the controversial Kemp-Roth tax cut proposal that would cut personal income tax rates by 30 percent over a three-year period. As *Newsweek* magazine put it in its March 2, 1981, issue, "Reagan thus gambled the future—his own, his party's, and in some measure the nation's—on a perilous and largely untested new course called supply-side economics."

Many prominent economists warned that to follow the plan President Reagan had put forth would lead to huge budget deficits and could prove disastrous for the economy. But, despite such warnings, the Reagan Economic Program was put into effect. The President had been elected by an enormous margin and he felt he had a mandate from the people to do whatever he thought was best. Apparently, the majority of Americans agreed, and the Congress—which was controlled by the Democrats at the time—enacted the Reagan proposals into law.

The results of the Reagan-Bush economic policies can be seen in Table 5. In just a little more than five years, our government doubled the national debt. And instead of the promised balanced budget by 1984, the federal government ran a budget *deficit* of $185.7 billion in fiscal year 1984. In 1992, the last of the Reagan-Bush years, the deficit was $340.5 billion, and the national debt was more than $4 trillion! Although it had taken this nation more than 200 years to accumulate the first $1 trillion of national debt in late 1981, it took only 12 years to quadruple it.

Ronald Reagan, the great communicator, had the charisma to get reelected despite the poor performance of the economy and the huge deficits. He was often referred to as the "Teflon" president, because very little seemed to stick to him personally. He had a way of deflecting the responsibility for problems onto other people. And, as the

TABLE 5

FEDERAL ON-BUDGET DEFICITS (-) OR SURPLUSES (+)
AND NATIONAL DEBT, FISCAL YEARS 1981-2003

(In Billions Of Dollars)

Year	On-budget Deficit (-) or Surplus (+)	National Debt at End of Period
1981	-74.0	994.8
1982	-120.1	1,137.3
1983	-208.0	1,371.7
1984	-185.7	1,564.7
1985	-221.7	1,817.5
1986	-238.0	2,120.6
1987	-169.3	2,346.1
1988	-194.0	2,601.3
1989	-205.2	2,868.0
1990	-277.8	3,206.6
1991	-321.6	3,598.5
1992	-340.5	4,002.1
1993	-300.5	4,351.4
1994	-258.9	4,643.7
1995	-226.4	4,921.0
1996	-174.1	5,181.9
1997	-103.4	5,369.7
1998	-30.0	5,478.7
1999	+1.9	5,606.1
2000	+86.6	5,629.0
2001	-33.4	5,770.3
2002	-317.5	6,198.4
2003*	-467.6	6,752.0

Source: Economic Report of the President, 2003
*Estimates

THE ON-BUDGET, OFF-BUDGET, AND UNIFIED BUDGET.

The on-budget of the United States is essentially what most people think of as the "operating budget." It includes all receipts and expenditures for government operations except those involving the Social Security Trust Fund.

The off-budget is primarily the Social Security budget. Technically, the United States Postal Service is also legally designated as "off-budget." However, since the Postal Service must maintain an approximately balanced budget in its operations, we can essentially equate the off-budget deficit or surplus with that of the Social Security system.

The on-budget deficit or surplus is a measure of whether the government is operating in the red or in the black, and the off-budget deficit or surplus is a measure of the solvency of the Social Security system.

The unified budget is a device for combining the on-budget and off-budget revenues and expenditures. It counts the entire revenue received by the government, including Social Security revenue, and the total expenditures of the government, including Social Security benefit payments. The unified budget tends to mask the true size of the on-budget deficits by using Social Security surpluses to offset on-budget deficits.

Prior to the 1983 Social Security tax increases, designed to build up a reserve for the retirement of the baby boomers, the Social Security program operated primarily on a "pay-as-you-go" basis which meant that each year the fund collected just about as much revenue as it paid out. Therefore, the Social Security fund had an approximately balanced budget every year, so that adding it to the on-budget did not distort the on-budget deficit very much.

As a result of the 1983 tax increases, the Social Security fund began running larger and larger annual surpluses that were supposed to go into the reserve. However, by combining the on-budget and off-budget into the unified budget, these Social Security surpluses masked the true size of the on-budget deficits, and ultimately exaggerated the size of the true surpluses that occurred in 1999 and 2000.

The unified-budget device has helped politicians pull off the fraud of using Social Security revenue for general government spending.

economy faltered and the huge budget deficits caused the national debt to skyrocket, Reagan would repeat over and over, "The economy has never been healthier, it has never been stronger." The statements were, of course, untrue, because the economy and the federal budget both suffered severely from the Reagan economic policies.

As Reagan's vice president, George Herbert Walker Bush inherited enough goodwill from his association with Reagan to get elected to a first term. However, Bush lacked Reagan's charisma and was on probation with the American voters from the day he took office. If he were to have any chance of being reelected to a second term, he would have to turn the economy around. And, given the fact that he had, during the 1980 primaries, referred to Reagan's economic proposals as voodoo economics that would lead to disaster, many observers hoped that Bush would abandon Reaganomics and return to more traditional economic policies. But Bush continued with the same failed economic policies that had done so much harm to the economy and to the federal budget under Reagan.

Bush's failure to chart a new course with regard to economic policies cost him any chance of reelection. Although Bush was riding so high in the public opinion polls after the Gulf War that most of the strongest Democratic potential challengers chose not to even run, his poor handling of the economy caused him to lose the presidency to a little-known governor from Arkansas, Bill Clinton.

Clinton promised to reduce the federal budget deficits, and once elected, he pushed through Congress a deficit reduction package that included both cuts in spending and higher taxes. Every Republican member of Congress opposed the Clinton plan, and not a single Republican, in either the House or the Senate, voted for it. It was only with Vice President Gore's tie-breaking vote that the legislation squeezed through the Senate, allowing President Clinton to sign it into law.

Republicans cried out, almost in unison, the warning that if the Clinton plan was adopted, both the economy and the federal budget would be seriously damaged. After 12 years of failed Reaganomics, the

Many people confuse the national debt and budget deficits. These two terms are very different although they are related.

Each year the government collects revenue in the form of tax receipts, and it also spends money in the form of government expenditures. If government expenditures are exactly equal to tax revenue, there is a balanced budget. This means that there is neither a budget surplus nor a budget deficit for that year.

If the government collects more tax revenue than it spends during any year, there is a budget surplus. However, if the government spends more money than it collects in tax revenue, there is a budget deficit.

How can the government spend more than it takes in? It does so in the same way that individuals and businesses spend more than their income. The government borrows money when it chooses to spend more in a given year than its income. Whenever an individual borrows money, that person's debt goes up.

The same is true of the government. Whenever the government borrows money to cover deficits in its budget, the national debt goes up.

EXAMPLE:

$5,770.3 billion—national debt at the end of fiscal year 2001
+   317.5 billion—deficit for fiscal year 2002
= $6,087.8 billion—national debt at end of fiscal year 2002.

The $317.5 billion that must be borrowed to cover the deficit for fiscal year 2002 must be added onto the national debt. (Actually the national debt will go up by more than the amount of the deficit because of other factors and bookkeeping procedures.)

ANY TIME THAT THE GOVERNMENT RUNS AN ANNUAL BUDGET DEFICIT, THE AMOUNT OF THAT DEFICIT MUST BE ADDED TO THE NATIONAL DEBT.

Republicans were still opposed to returning to traditional economic policies, and they predicted that the Clinton plan would be disastrous if enacted.

After eight years in office, Clinton turned over the presidency to George W. Bush on January 20, 2001. During the last year of the Clinton presidency, the unemployment rate was the lowest it had been in 30 years, 22 million new jobs had been created, the poverty rate was the lowest in 20 years, and there was a non-Social Security surplus of $86.6 billion, compared to the whopping $340.5 billion deficit during the last year of George Herbert Walker Bush's presidency. In short, both the budget and the economy were in great shape when Clinton turned over the reins of power to George W. Bush.

By the third year of the George W. Bush presidency, the unemployment rate had risen to 6 percent, and 2 million jobs had been lost. Instead of the $86.6 billion surplus during the last Clinton year, the non-Social Security budget ran a whopping $317.5 billion deficit in 2002, and a deficit of $467.6 billion was projected for 2003. In addition, George W. Bush had already added $732 billion to the national debt, only slightly less than the $995 billion added to the debt by the first 39 presidents combined. According to Congressional Budget Office official projections, during George W. Bush's first four years, the national debt will go up by $1,164.8 billion (or $1.16 trillion), without counting the cost of the war with Iraq. All of these projections are based on only the tax cuts enacted at the beginning of the Bush presidency. The additional $350 billion tax cut enacted in May 2003 just makes the projections a great deal more dire.

IN SUMMARY, ECONOMIC ILLITERACY is one of the greatest threats to the future of the American economy. Because of widespread economic illiteracy, it is possible for politicians to engage in major economic malpractice without being held accountable by the voters. And America has suffered a great deal because of that economic malpractice.

The Great Depression of the 1930s demonstrates just how big a price the nation can pay for failure to follow sound economic policies.

However, since modern economics was still young and untested in the 1930s, political leaders of that period can be excused to some degree on the basis that they did not really know very much about the economy.

The economic malpractice during the Johnson administration and during the Reagan-Bush years is an entirely different matter. President Johnson, and Presidents Reagan and Bush, ignored the advice of their own economic advisers in order to pursue political goals. America paid a terrible price, and millions of Americans suffered needlessly because of the failure of these three presidents to follow sound economic policies. Yet, in 2001, George W. Bush, knowing the terrible consequences of the economic policies of his father and Ronald Reagan, recklessly launched the nation on a new round of Reaganomics in order to achieve his short-term political goal of enacting large tax cuts mostly for the rich.

CHAPTER FOUR

Economic Malpractice During the Reagan-Bush Years

∿

Let us cut through the fog for a moment. The answer to a government that's too big is to stop feeding its growth . . . The massive national debt which we accumulated is the result of the government's high spending diet . . . Well, it's time to change the diet and to change it in the right way . . . These policies will make our economy stronger, and the stronger economy will balance the budget which we're committed to do by 1984.

—Ronald Reagan [April 28, 1981]

IN 1981, PRESIDENT REAGAN abandoned Keynesian economics, which had been the predominant body of economic theory for nearly half a century, and launched the nation in a new direction based on a new, untested theory. It was called supply-side economics. This new theory, which received most of its support from politicians and other noneconomists, had the support of only a very few professionally trained economists.

Usually, new economic theories require years of debate and testing before they stand a chance of being implemented as part of government economic policy, even when they are the product of some of the greatest minds in the field. But because the ideas of the supply-side supporters were so compatible with the political philosophy of Ronald

Reagan, the new, untested theory was to become the cornerstone of Reagan's economic policy.

Most professional economists had probably never heard the term "supply-side economics" until Ronald Reagan announced his support for it in the 1980 primary campaign. I had a Ph.D. degree in economics and had been teaching the subject to college students for more than a dozen years at the time Reagan introduced the concept to the world. Yet, I had never seen any reference to the concept in any of the professional literature, and it was not included in any textbook I had ever used. There is good reason for this. The theory almost came out of nowhere. Robert Merry and Kenneth Bacon stated in a February 18, 1981 *Wall Street Journal* article, "Capturing the Executive Branch of government was an amazing victory for the supply-side movement, which hardly existed a mere eight years ago." And so it was. Never before had an economic theory so new, so untested, and with so little support from professional economists as a whole, been accepted and pushed by the federal government.

According to Merry and Bacon, supply-side economics became a political movement when the ideas of Arthur Laffer of the University of Southern California, and Robert Mundell of Columbia University, captured the imagination of Jude Wanniski, an editorial writer for the *Wall Street Journal*, who reportedly sought receptive Washington politicians and finally found one in Representative Jack Kemp of New York. In 1977, Representative Kemp, along with Senator William Roth of Delaware, coauthored the Kemp-Roth Bill to slash individual income tax rates by 30 percent over a three-year period. Mr. Kemp then reportedly set out to convert Mr. Reagan, whom he considered the most receptive of the potential presidents.

The ideas and objectives of the supply-siders were very compatible with Mr. Reagan's own political philosophy, so it was not difficult to convert him to the new economic theories. Thus, Reagan's pledge to support passage of the Kemp-Roth Bill and call for a 30 percent cut in tax rates over a three-year period became the most popular promise of his campaign and undoubtedly played a major role in his election.

Supply-side economists emphasized the interrelationship between the total supply of goods and services and the government's taxing and spending policies. They believed that tax rates had become so high that there was a disincentive to work or produce. Some also argued that subsidies to the poor were so generous that they discouraged the poor from increasing their earnings for fear their government aid would be reduced.

President Reagan's proposed 30 percent cut in tax rates over a three-year period was based on the argument that such a tax cut would result in a substantial increase in the total supply of goods and services produced. The argument was based on the belief that high tax rates prompted many individuals to take more lengthy vacations, accept less overtime work, and retire earlier than they would if tax rates were substantially lower. In addition, the supply-siders argued that the high tax rates discouraged business people from pursuing promising but risky investment opportunities because, even if they were successful, the government would take much of their profit.

These beliefs led supply-siders to argue that a massive tax cut such as Reagan proposed would lead to more revenue, not less. Here is where the theories left the real world and entered fantasyland. The American people were being told that they could have their cake and eat it too, and they loved it. According to Reagan, he could cut tax rates by 30 percent and collect more government revenue than before the tax cut. In fact, President Reagan promised that if Congress would just enact his proposal, the federal budget would be balanced by 1984 and he would simultaneously reduce both unemployment and inflation.

Congress did enact the president's economic program, including the tax-cut proposal, which had been reduced (at the request of Budget Director David Stockman) from a 30 percent cut to a 25 percent cut in personal income tax rates over a three-year period. However, the country soon learned that the promised simultaneous reduction in inflation and unemployment rates was not to be. Inflation did come down, as the economy plunged into the worst recession in half a century. The civilian unemployment rate climbed to 10.7 percent in December 1982, the highest rate since the Great Depression of the 1930s. Millions of Americans lost their jobs, and the annual civilian unemployment rate remained above 9.5 percent for both 1982 and 1983.

As the economy recovered from the severe recession, President Reagan argued that his economic policies were working, and the economy was headed toward true and lasting prosperity. On the surface, things did look encouraging; the unemployment rate was gradually declining, and inflation was remaining low, but a huge cloud hung over the optimistic forecasts: federal budget deficits of unprecedented size and the rapid growth in the national debt.

The president had promised in 1980 that his policies would lead to a balanced budget by 1984. Instead, the federal budget deficits soared from $73.8 billion in fiscal 1980 to a record $221.7 billion in fiscal 1985. Reagan added more to the national debt in six years than the combined debt all presidents from George Washington through Jimmy Carter had added over a period of nearly 200 years.

Nations, like individuals, cannot live beyond their means indefinitely. While much of the borrowed money came from Americans who invested in government securities, substantial amounts of foreign capital were used to finance the huge budget deficits. Between 1981 and 1986, the United States was transformed from the world's largest lender to the world's largest borrower.

Why were the basic economic problems allowed to grow to such disastrous proportions? The primary reason was that, for the first time in modern history, an American president chose to ignore almost totally the advice of professional economists, both inside and outside the administration. Reagan listened only to those whose advice was compatible with Reaganomics, and simply ignored the rest. It would have been bad enough if the president had dismissed the advice of only the outside economists who disagreed with his policies, but he would not even listen to his own handpicked economic advisers.

The Employment Act of 1946 required the president to appoint a Council of Economic Advisers so that he would always have close access to the advice of some of the best professional economists in the country. Thus, President Reagan did appoint three economists to his Council of Economic Advisers. Unfortunately, however, he chose not to listen to their advice; instead, he allowed people with little or no professional training in economics to formulate his economic policies.

When Murray Weidenbaum, Reagan's first chairman of the Council of Economic Advisers, resigned early in the administration, the President had the opportunity to search the nation for his type of economist as Weidenbaum's replacement. Finally, in 1982, he selected Martin Feldstein, a Harvard economist, as his new chairman.

Mr. Feldstein took his appointment seriously, and he expected to influence economic policy within the administration. He immediately began to warn the president that something had to be done about the gigantic federal budget deficits. However, Feldstein soon learned that he had been appointed only to fill the position, and that his advice was not going to be taken seriously.

As early as 1983, Feldstein had said, "If Congress doesn't act soon to cut future deficits, interest rates will remain high and weaken the economy. Future back-to-back $200 billion deficits will increase the national debt by an additional $1 trillion over the next few years, eventually forcing the government to implement drastic spending cuts and tax increases."

When Feldstein warned of the deficit dangers in the 1984 Economic Report of the President, Treasury Secretary, Donald Regan, a noneconomist who was playing a major role in economic policy-making, told Congress, "As far as I'm concerned, you can throw it [the Economic Report] away." Feldstein had stated that the deficits, if not curtailed soon, could devastate the nation's economy. He had argued that taxes should be raised as a way of reducing the projected $180 billion fiscal 1985 deficit which as it turned out was actually $221.7 billion.

No one was listening, and when Feldstein, out of frustration, began giving public speeches on the subject of the dangerous deficits, he was ordered to submit his speeches to the White House for prior approval before he delivered them. Feldstein was scheduled to appear on an

ABC news show on Sunday February 5, 1984, when he was ordered by the White House to cancel the scheduled appearance because his comments might embarrass the administration.

When Feldstein left the administration in 1984, President Reagan then proposed abolishing the Council of Economic Advisers because he felt it served no useful purpose. Of course, Congress had created the Council of Economic Advisers with the Employment Act of 1946 to ensure that all future presidents would have the benefit of the best professionally trained economists available in order to avoid major economic policy mistakes. President Reagan, who had demonstrated repeatedly throughout his administration through his speeches and actions that he had almost no understanding of how the American economy operated, wanted no part of any such arrangement. To formulate the economic policy of the nation, he would rely on noneconomists who shared his political philosophy.

In the early years of the administration, the chief architects of Reagan's economic policy were Treasury Secretary Donald Regan and Budget Director David Stockman. Mr. Regan, who was the former head of the Merrill Lynch stock brokerage firm, had business experience, but he was not an economist. Many people who are quite successful at business have very little understanding of how the national economy operates. Budget Director Stockman, who was probably the chief architect of economic policy in the early days, had absolutely no formal training in economics. Yet despite the warnings of many outside prominent economists—including recipients of the Nobel Prize in economics—as well as his own handpicked Harvard economist, Martin Feldstein, President Reagan allowed noneconomists to formulate national economic policy. The damage done to the economy by these people will be felt for a long time to come.

In order to understand why a president would ignore the advice of most professional economists and allow noneconomists to formulate economic policy, one must understand that the goals of the "Reagan Revolution" were more political than economic in nature. President Reagan came to Washington determined to reverse the political direction that this nation had been following for 40 years. The new president had hated the growth in government social programs that had evolved during that time, and he was determined to move the nation in a new direction.

Reagan wanted to reduce the size of the federal government and the role it played in the American economy. He was determined to reduce spending on social programs and increase spending on national defense. And he was determined to reduce taxes, especially for the very wealthy. When supply-side advocates approached him with the Kemp-Roth tax cut proposal and promised that it would lead to a stronger economy, as well as accomplish his political objectives, the president couldn't have been happier. From then on, mainstream economists and mainstream economic policies would not have much of a role to play in the Reagan administration. If the economic advice was not compatible with the goals of the Reagan Revolution, it was to be ignored. In other words, the president was far more interested in accomplishing his political goals than he was in pursuing sound economic policies.

A primary goal of the Reagan tax cuts was to reduce government spending. He thought that if there was less government revenue available there would have to be sharp reductions in spending. Somehow, he had underestimated how easy it would be to just borrow funds to replace the revenue lost from the tax cut. In his first televised address to the nation, on February 5, 1981, Reagan declared: "There were always those who told us that taxes couldn't be cut until spending was reduced. Well, you know we can lecture our children about extravagance until we run out of voice and breath. Or we can cut their extravagance by simply reducing their allowance." Reagan seemed to think that he could cut government spending by simply reducing taxes and thus cutting back on the government's "allowance."

In early January of 1981, Budget Director David Stockman, who was 34 years old and lacked any formal training in economics, began to formulate plans for the first Reagan budget. When Stockman and his staff fed the data of the proposed Reagan economic program into a computer that was programmed as a model of the nation's economic behavior, and instructed it to estimate the impact of Reagan's program on the federal budget, he was shocked. The computer predicted that if the president went ahead with his promised three-year tax reduction and his increase in defense spending, the Reagan Administration would be faced with a series of federal budget deficits without precedent. The projections ranged from an $82 billion deficit in 1982 to $116 billion in 1984—the year the president had promised to balance the budget. Stockman knew that if those were the numbers included in President Reagan's first budget message the following month, the financial markets would panic and Congress would be unlikely to approve the budget.

The young Stockman decided that the assumptions programmed into the computer by earlier economists were not correct, so he and his team discarded orthodox premises of how the economy would behave and reprogrammed the computer with new assumptions that would give them the projected 1984 balanced budget the president had promised. Later, the nonpartisan Congressional Budget Office projected continuing large budget deficits—not a balanced budget by 1984. When President Reagan was asked by reporters why the two sets of projections were so different, he charged that the Congressional Budget Office and members of Congress endorsing the CBO projections were trying to shoot down his economic program by using "phony" figures.

Phony figures were indeed being used, but not by the CBO. Of course, the Congress and the public had no way of knowing at the time that Stockman had rigged the OMB computer to project a balanced budget for 1984. It was not until the publication of the infamous article, "The Education of David Stockman," by William Greider in the December 1981 issue of *The Atlantic Monthly* that the public learned the whole story.

Much was learned about the early days of the Reagan Administration from that article which almost cost Stockman his job. According to Greider, when Stockman's appointment as budget director first seemed likely, he had agreed to meet with Greider, then an assistant managing editor at the *Washington Post*, from time to time and relate, off the record, his private account of the great political struggle ahead. The particulars of these conversations were not to be reported until later, after the president's program had been approved by Congress. Stockman and Greider met for regular conversations over breakfast for eight months, and their conversations provided the basis for Greider's article in *The Atlantic Monthly*.

When the article was published it became a political bombshell. In addition to revealing the computer-rigging to get budget projections that could be sold to Congress, Stockman asserted that the supply-side theory was not a new economic theory at all but just new language and a new argument for the doctrine of the old Republican orthodoxy known as "trickle down" economics. Basically, this doctrine holds that the government should give tax cuts to the top brackets; the wealthiest individuals and the largest enterprises, and let the good effects "trickle down" through the economy to reach everyone else. According to Stockman, when one stripped away the new rhetoric emphasizing across-the-board cuts, the supply-side theory was really just new clothes for the unpopular doctrine of the old Republican orthodoxy. Greider quoted Stockman as saying, "It's kind of hard to sell 'trickle down,' so the supply-side formula was the only way to get a tax policy that was really 'trickle down.' Supply-side is 'trickle down' theory."

In the same article, Stockman added, "The hard part of the supply-side tax cut is dropping the top rate from 73 to 50 percent—the rest of it is a secondary matter. The original argument was that the top bracket was too high, and that's having the most devastating effect on the economy. Then, the general argument was that, in order to make this palatable as a political matter, you had to bring down all brackets. But, I mean, Kemp-Roth was always a Trojan horse to bring down the top rate."

Many people were misled by the 25 percent cut in personal income tax rates that was enacted during the first year of the Reagan presidency. Many thought it meant a 25 percent cut in the amount of taxes each individual paid. But this wasn't true. People who were in the 70 percent bracket, which was cut to 50 percent, saved $20 on each $100 of taxable income. However, a person who was in the 16 percent bracket would have his or her tax rate cut from 16 percent to 12 percent, and would save only $4 on each $100 of taxable income. In other words, the tax cut benefited the rich to a much greater extent than it did the poor. In fact, because of the substantial cuts in programs that benefited primarily the poor, most poor people were actually hurt by the tax cut.

Many programs designed to help the poor were cut or eliminated to pay for the big tax cut, much of which went to the wealthy. Whether this is right or wrong involves value judgments. However, many Americans who like to think of this country as a fair and compassionate nation feel there was little evidence of concern for the problems of the poor in the Reagan economic program.

On January 27, 1982, in his State of the Union address, Ronald Reagan gave his perception of the state of the economy after one year of Reaganomics. Below are excerpts from that speech.

... When I visited this chamber last year as a newcomer to Washington, critical of past policies which I believe had failed, I proposed a new spirit of partnership between this Congress and the Administration and between Washington and our state and local governments.

... It's my duty to report to you tonight on the progress that we have made in our relations with other nations, on the foundation we have laid for our economic recovery and, finally, on a bold and spirited initiative that I believe can change the face of American government and make it again the servant of the people.

... The situation at this time last year was truly ominous ... Late in 1981, we sank into the present recession ...

... This time, however, things are different. We have an economic program in place completely different from the artificial quick-fixes of the past. It calls for a reduction of the rate of increase in government spending, and . . . [w]e've just implemented the first and smallest phase of a three-year tax-rate reduction designed to stimulate the economy and create jobs . . . If we had not acted as we did, things would be far worse for all Americans than they are today.

Together, we not only cut the increase in government spending nearly in half, we brought about the largest tax reductions and the most sweeping changes in our tax structure since the beginning of this century.

. . . The only alternative being offered to this economic program is a return to the policies that gave us a trillion-dollar debt, runaway inflation, runaway interest rates and unemployment.

The doubters would have us turn back the clock with tax increases that would offset the personal tax-rate reductions already passed by Congress.

Raise present taxes to cut future deficits, they tell us. Well, I don't believe we should buy that argument . . . Raising taxes won't balance the budget. It will encourage more Government spending and less private investment . . .

So I will not ask you to try to balance the budget on the backs of the American taxpayers. I will seek no tax increases this year and I have no intention of retreating from our basic program of tax relief. I promised the American people to bring their tax rates down and keep them down to provide them incentives to rebuild our economy, to save, to invest in America's future. I will stand by my word.

Reagan was patting himself on the back a little prematurely. He minimizes the seriousness of the recession because, "This time . . . things are different. We have an economic program in place completely different from the artificial quick-fixes of the past."

Well, the economic program in place didn't work very well. Unemployment rates soared to their highest levels since the Great Depression of the 1930s. During Reagan's first four-year term, the average annual unemployment rate was 8.6 percent—7.6 percent in 1981, 9.7 percent in 1982, 9.6 percent in 1983, and 7.5 percent in 1984. At no other time since the Great Depression of the 1930s had the unemployment rate ever been as high as 8.6 percent even for a single year, let alone for a 4-year average.

If we look at Mr. Reagan's full 8-year presidency, the average annual unemployment rate is 7.5 percent. Since the Great Depression, only in 1975 and 1976 , during the Ford presidency, has the unemployment rate been as high, in even a single year, as Reagan's 8-year average unemployment rate.

The severe recession of 1981-82 did not have to happen. It was caused by government policies. If the president had implemented the planned 10 percent tax cut in January and called on the Federal Reserve (Fed) to pursue an easier-money policy, it is my belief that there would not have been a recession and all the suffering that accompanied it. Of course, the economy could not have withstood the planned two additional 10 percent cuts in the two succeeding years without problems of large deficits. But the first year's planned 10 percent tax cut was very much needed at the time to stimulate the economy.

As President Reagan ended his term of office he claimed that his administration had been one of prosperity. However, the record shows otherwise. *President Reagan had the worst unemployment record of any modern president.*

President Reagan tried to blame the high unemployment of the early years of his term on former President Jimmy Carter. Reagan claimed the economy was already in a recession when he took office. This is not true. The unemployment rate was 7.7 percent during the last year of the Ford Administration. President Carter added 10 million jobs to the economy during his four years in office, and the unemployment rate was reduced to 5.8 percent in 1979 before the economy entered a mild recession in January of 1980 that began driving unemployment back up. However, the rising unemployment did not last long. The recession hit bottom two months later, in March 1980, and the economy was expanding again and the unemployment rate declining when President Reagan took office. However, the economy was very fragile, having just come out of a recession. It was therefore extremely important that the proper economic policies be followed to prevent the economy from slipping into a new recession.

The policies of the Reagan administration played a major role in the severe recession of 1981–82. The president called upon the Federal Reserve System to pursue a tight-money policy, he cut domestic spending, and he failed to implement his promised first-year, 10 percent cut in tax rates, which was to have been retroactive to January 1, 1981. The fragile economy could not withstand such tight constraints. Budget Director David Stockman, who had begun to worry about forthcoming deficits, convinced the president to reduce his first-year tax cut from 10 percent to 5 percent, and delay its implementation until October 1, 1981. Thus, instead of the 10 percent cut in tax rates for the entire year that had been planned, there was a cut of only 5 percent, and it was in effect for only the last 3 months of the year. This translates into a 1.25 percent average tax cut for the entire year instead of the planned 10 percent cut. These tight fiscal constraints, combined with the tight-money policy, plunged the economy into the worst recession since the Great Depression of the 1930s, causing millions of Americans to lose their jobs.

President Reagan claimed that he brought inflation under control. However, Reagan could not take credit for reducing inflation unless he was willing to accept the blame for the recession. The inflation rate came down for the following reasons.

- First and foremost, there is no surer way to reduce inflation than to throw the economy into a severe recession. With aggregate demand falling, it is difficult for prices to rise. As more and more people become unemployed and lose their spending power, sellers are forced to reduce their prices, or at least to stop raising them, in order to make sales.
- Second, much of the inflation of the 1970s was caused by soaring energy prices. The price of crude oil rose from $3 a barrel to $33 a barrel during the period 1973 to 1980. This

caused an increase in the price of almost everything, because energy makes up a part of the production cost and much of the transportation cost of most products. Just as President Reagan took office a glut in world oil supplies developed, making it impossible for crude oil prices to rise further.

• Even if oil prices had remained at a steady level of $33 per barrel, there would have been no further upward pressures on prices resulting from the energy crisis. But crude oil prices actually dropped substantially during the Reagan administration, helping to offset price increases of other items and keep the inflation rate low.

The national debt doubled from $1 trillion to $2 trillion during the first six years of the Reagan presidency, and was more than $2.6 trillion when Reagan left office. However, things were to get much worse during the next four years under President Bush.

On January 24, 1990, President George H. W. Bush held a news conference in which he was put on the defensive for his use of Social Security taxes to fund general government operating expenses. Reporters asked the president a number of pointed questions, and he certainly had ample opportunity to deny, or try to justify, the use of these surpluses. But the president evaded every single question, in essence leaving the impression that all the harsh criticism was valid. The following are excerpts from the president's news conference.

Q. Mr. President, over the last few years there have been large increases in the Social Security tax. And even though it's a regressive tax, people supported it, or swallowed it, because they were told that that was necessary to make the system solvent for the next generation. But now everyone is finding out that, in fact, that money isn't there any longer, that it's been used for debt reduction. Given the fact that people are now realizing that this is happening, do you think it's fair to ask them to continue to pay this increased tax for even 1 month longer?

A. The Commission that reformed Social Security was well-aware of what you've just talked about. They considered it. I think the Commission included Mr. Moynihan—I may be mistaken, but I think it did. And they considered this point. And we will have some innovative suggestions as we go along here as to how to compensate for this understandable concern on the part of some. But for now, for this year, we will not alter the recommendations of that bipartisan commission.

Q. Could I just briefly—do you feel that this increase was sold to people under false premises?

A. No, because I think these were intelligent people wrestling with a very, very difficult problem, and I can't accuse them of selling the Commission conclusion as under false cover.

Q. Well, as you know, the budget deficit has been coming down over the past few years solely because the Social Security surplus has been rising. In fact, your own budget projections show $200 billion a year deficits in the indefinite future when you remove the Social Security surplus. Given the fact that you have such a large deficit in every other program, when will you and the Congress stop both bickering and accountant gimmicks and deal with this problem that the American public has said for a decade . . .

A. Thank you for the endorsement of our approach, Owen. We would urge that we stop bickering and go forward with the proposal that we come out with, that I think will begin to address itself to Maureen's question, that is very sound. And nobody's trying to conceal the fact that the Social Security Trust Fund is operating at a surplus. . . .

Q. Well, wait. If I could follow, sir: Your own budget proposal that you will unveil on Monday, which shows a $64 billion deficit, in fact, if you remove Social Security, would be closer to $150 billion. Is that not correct?

A. But you're making the old argument of taking the Social Security Trust Fund off budget. And at this juncture we're not prepared to do that. But wait until you see the detail, and I hope the American people will see something here that begins to address itself to these fundamentals that I think are properly being asked about.

Reporters turned to other subject categories at this point, but near the end of the news conference, Social Security taxes came up once again.

Q. Mr. President, another question that's been raised about the Moynihan proposal is the fairness of the tax system. Over the past decade, even as income tax has come down for high-paid people, Social Security taxes have gone up, mostly for lower and middle-income people. Do you think that's fair?

A. Well, look, if we were all starting over, I think we could fine-tune the entire tax system. We're not starting over. And I think that system has been in and out over the years, basically a pretty fair system. . . .

Q. But, sir, some of your favorite economists in think tanks say that the Social Security tax acts as a great disincentive to work and to employing people.

A. Yes

Q. Doesn't that serve the same end?

A. Well, I think that's a legitimate complaint about some of it, and that's one of the reasons I favor holding the line on taxes. And one of the reasons I oppose Moynihan is I think it's a disguise for increased taxes around the corner. And I don't want to see the benefits of Social Security cut. It is odd that a Republican president, often accused by political opponents in an election year, is the one that is protecting the sanctity of the Social Security benefits. And I would say to those out around the country: Take a hard look now—don't let that rabbit be pulled out of the hat by 1 hand and 25 other rabbits dumped on you in another. This is a very complicated situation, and this is a sleight of hand operation here. . . .

The president had ample opportunity during that news conference to explain why he was using Social Security money for other government programs and to mask the true size of the budget deficits. He also had the opportunity to deny the fact that he was indeed engaged in such fraudulent behavior, and the opportunity to offer some explanation that might justify what he was doing. But the president neither denied the accusation nor gave any justification for misappropriating the Social Security funds.

In essence, President George Bush admitted to the misuse of Social Security funds by totally evading the questions. He also demonstrated an almost total lack of knowledge about the Social Security Commission; if he wasn't sure whether Senator Moynihan, one of the commission's most vocal members, was even on the Commission, how could he possibly have known in depth what its recommendations were?

Later that day, Senator Moynihan responded to the president's accusation that he was engaged in a sleight of hand operation on the Senate floor.

Mr. MOYNIHAN. I thank my distinguished, gallant, generous colleague from New Jersey for giving me this opportunity.

Mr. President.

I rise for a painful purpose—to state my disappointment in the remarks made by the president this morning at his press conference in response to questions concerning my legislation to return the Social Security System to pay-as-you-go financing. I introduced the bill yesterday in the company of a number of colleagues, having said on December 29 that I would do so.

Mr. President, there is no "sleight of hand" involved whatever. I do not see that there was any need to make such a characterization. If there is a problem of dissimulation, I would suggest it resides with the present practice of using Social Security trust funds as general revenues. My distinguished friend, the Republican Senator from Pennsylvania, Senator Heinz, has used a very direct word for this. He says it is called "embezzlement."

Moynihan was the target of much criticism from Republicans for daring to force the government into being honest about its finances. On April 4, 1990, Tom Ridge, then a congressman from Pennsylvania, requested permission to address the house with regard to the Moynihan proposal.

Mr. RIDGE. Mr. Speaker, I rise today to express my opposition to Senator Moynihan's plan to cut the Social Security payroll tax and to express my surprise that the Democratic National Committee endorses it.

Mr. Speaker, this proposal endangers the Social Security trust fund reserves and could lead to substantially higher taxes when current obligations become due. The Moynihan proposal puts the future stability and integrity of the Social Security system in doubt and only creates problems where solutions are needed. It is unfair to future generations to eliminate reserves created for them and paid for by them.

Mr. Speaker, I do not know why the Democrats would endorse such a plan eagerly. Maybe they simply saw a surplus that they could not figure out a way to spend.

We may not know why the Democrats may want to threaten Social Security, but the American people should know that President Bush and the Republicans will try to do all they can to keep those Democratic hands off those Social Security benefits.

This was the ultimate in political spin and character assassination. From its very beginning, the Social Security system was opposed by many Republicans, and counting on Republicans to protect Social Security would be like placing a fox in the chicken house to guard the chickens. Social Security was always the Democrats' baby, and some Democrats spent their entire political careers trying to protect it. Senator Moynihan was one such person. He was without doubt one of the greatest friends that Social Security had ever had. He served on the 1982 Commission to reform Social Security, and he served on President George W. Bush's Social Security Commission. It was outrageous for Ridge, who was a participant in President George Bush's Social Security fraud, to deceive the American public by claiming that President Bush and the Republicans were trying to save the Social Security reserves, every dollar of which had already been embezzled.

One accomplishment of the Reagan-Bush years that is very dear to the hearts of conservatives was the reduction in revenue that necessitated smaller government. Although Reaganomics is usually associated with the theories of supply-side economics, a more accurate description of Reaganomics is: the policies based primarily on the personal economic position, beliefs, and assumptions of Ronald Reagan. When the supply-siders tried to convince Reagan to endorse their plan for a 30 percent cut in income tax rates, they had no problem at all. The big tax cut was totally in line with Reagan's number one goal—to reduce the size of the federal government.

Reagan said over and over that the economic problems of America were the result of too much government; he wanted to trim it as much as possible, and he seemed to believe that if taxes were cut severely, there would be a corresponding cut in federal spending. In Reagan's first inaugural address he said:

... great as our tax burden is, it has not kept pace with public spending. For decades, we have piled deficit upon deficit, mortgaging our future and our children's future for the temporary convenience of the present. To continue this long trend is to guarantee tremendous social, cultural, political, and economic upheavals.

You and I, as individuals, can, by borrowing, live beyond our means, but for only a limited period of time. Why, then, should we think that collectively, as a nation, we are not bound by that same limitation?

... It is my intention to curb the size and influence of the federal establishment and to demand recognition of the distinction between the powers granted to the federal government and those reserved to the states or to the people ... It is no coincidence that our present troubles parallel and are proportionate to the intervention and intrusion in our lives that result from unnecessary and excessive growth of government.

With the benefit of hindsight, we can now see just how contradictory Reagan's words and actions were. When he said, "FOR DECADES, WE HAVE PILED DEFICIT UPON DEFICIT, MORTGAGING OUR FUTURE AND OUR CHILDREN'S FUTURE FOR THE TEMPORARY CONVENIENCE OF THE PRESENT," a reasonable person would likely conclude that Reagan was being critical of large government deficits. One would then further conclude that Reagan intended to follow policies that would result in smaller deficits. Instead, Reagan gave us budget deficits of a magnitude not even imagined in the past, and during his eight years as president he almost tripled the size of the national debt.

Prior to Reagan's presidency, we had never had a budget deficit as high as $100 billion, and only two years with deficits in the $70 billion range. In 1976, during the Ford administration, the deficit was $70.5 billion. In 1980, during the Carter administration, the deficit was $72.2 billion. Both of these deficits were primarily the result of economic recessions that reduced the government's tax revenue. The average annual deficit for the entire decade of the 1970s was only

$35.38 billion. These are the deficits that Reagan was so critical of—the ones he said had "mortgaged our future and our children's future."

The average deficit of $168.87 billion for the decade of the 1980s dwarfed the average deficit of $35.38 billion for the decade of the 1970s. The annual deficits soared under both President Reagan and President George Herbert Walker Bush. The 1982 deficit of $120.1 billion represented the first time in history that the deficit had topped the $100 billion mark. The very next year, in 1983, the deficit exceeded the $200 billion mark, weighing in at $208 billion.

The longer the Reagan economic policies were in place, the larger the budget deficits became. In 1992, the last year of the George H.W. Bush administration, the budget deficit was an astronomical $340 billion! The national debt, which was less than $1 trillion when Reagan assumed the presidency, had quadrupled to more than $4 trillion by the time George Bush turned over the reins of power to Bill Clinton.

Clinton pushed through a controversial deficit-reduction package without the vote of a single Republican member of Congress, amid outcries that his plan would devastate both the economy and the budget. But the budget deficits gradually and steadily declined throughout the Clinton years, finally resulting in a tiny surplus of $1.9 billion in 1999 and a sizable surplus of $86.6 billion in 2000.

Historians will have a difficult time explaining why the American voters (or more accurately, the United States Supreme Court) sent George W. Bush to replace Bill Clinton. George W. Bush is almost a carbon copy of Ronald Reagan in terms of the economic policies he advocates. Reaganomics failed miserably during the 12 years that Reagan and George Bush occupied the White House, and there was a turnaround only after Clinton took office and began reducing the size of the deficits. At the end of the Clinton administration, the economy had never been better. The unemployment rate was at a 30-year low, and the federal deficits had been transformed into an $86.6 billion surplus.

Bush introduced a new round of Reaganomics, and both the economy and the federal budget situation deteriorated rapidly. By the third year of George W. Bush's presidency, the unemployment rate was 6.4

percent, more than 2 million jobs had been lost, and the federal budget was out of control. The on-budget deficit for 2002 was $317.5 billion, and the projected deficit for fiscal 2003 was $467.6 billion. Deficits for 2004, and after, were projected at more than $500 billion per year.

In summary, before the introduction of Reaganomics, the nation had accumulated approximately $1 trillion in national debt throughout our entire history. Twelve years later, the debt had quadrupled. The economic malpractice of the Reagan-Bush years will have a negative impact for generations to come. American taxpayers are currently paying approximately $500 million per day in interest just on that portion of the debt accumulated during those 12 years, and this will continue in perpetuity.

CHAPTER FIVE

Clinton and a Return to Traditional Economic Policies

❧

As the President and congressional Democrats busily work on the biggest tax increase in the history of the world, the American people are watching, and they do not like what they see. . . . To put it simply, the Clinton tax increase promises to turn the American dream into a nightmare for millions of hardworking Americans.

—Senator Robert Dole, [June 30, 1993]

*A*S LITTLE AS A year before the 1992 election, the likelihood that a little-known governor from Arkansas would be elected president seemed almost nonexistent. President George Bush was riding so high in the polls that most of the leading potential Democratic challengers chose not to even enter the race. Bush had been the commander in chief in the Gulf War, the most decisive American military victory since World War II, and most observers believed that Bush would be unbeatable in 1992.

After a stormy primary campaign in a field of what most political experts considered "lightweight" candidates, Bill Clinton, then governor of Arkansas, was nominated as the 1992 Democratic candidate. Most observers expected Clinton to serve as the sacrificial lamb for the Democratic party, and thought the nomination was not worth having. Some of the losing candidates, and those would-be candidates who had chosen not to run, tended to just write off the 1992 election as a lost cause, and started thinking about 1996.

Bill Clinton, however, never saw himself as a sacrificial lamb, and he was determined to become the next president of the United States. The boy from Hope, Arkansas, who had once considered becoming a professional saxophone player, had set his sites on the White House when he was still in high school. As a delegate to Boys Nation, Clinton had met President John F. Kennedy in the White House Rose Garden, and the encounter had changed his life forever. He decided to enter a life of politics and public service, and he expected to return to the White House someday as president.

Despite his popularity as a wartime president, Bush soon discovered just how important the economy was to American voters. Ross Perot, a self-made billionaire, entered the race as a third-party candidate and ran a one-issue campaign on deficit reduction. Clinton hit hard on the deficit, but also emphasized the need for a major change in Washington. He convinced enough of the voters who were looking for change to vote for him to receive 43.3 percent of the popular vote compared to 37.7 percent for Bush and 19 percent for Perot. In terms of the electoral votes, the race wasn't even close. Clinton got 370 votes compared to Bush's 168.

Clinton had promised to reduce the deficit, and he was determined to do so, no matter how unpopular his prescription was with the established Washington politicians. He proposed a deficit reduction plan that included both major spending cuts and higher taxes. There was immediate stiff opposition to the plan because it included higher taxes. The Republican party had benefited immensely from the credit it got from the Reagan tax cuts, despite the fact that the Reagan cuts were the primary cause of the ongoing massive budget deficits. The Congressional Republicans were determined to block any effort to raise taxes.

The Republican doomsayers argued that passage of the Clinton economic plan would wreck the economy. House Minority Leader Robert H. Michel (R-IL), portrayed Clinton as a traditional tax-and-spend Democrat who was trying to obscure that truth with "the biggest propaganda campaign in recent political history." One House Republican said the Clinton budget was a "recipe for economic and fiscal disaster," and another one said the package "would put the economy in the gutter."

Congressman Dana Rohrabacher (R-CA) rose on the House floor and said, "Mr. Speaker, I rise in strong opposition to the Clinton tax increase, the largest tax increase in American history, which will hit the middle class, bring our economy to a standstill and in the end increase the deficit."

Republican Congressman Christopher Cox, also from California, was even more graphic in denouncing the Clinton plan. He said, "This is really the Dr. Kevorkian plan for our economy. It will kill jobs, kill businesses, and yes, kill even the higher tax revenues that these suicidal tax increasers hope to gain."

Senate Republicans were equally harsh in their denunciation of the Clinton economic plan. One of the most emotionally charged debates on the Clinton economic plan took place on the floor of the Senate on April 3, 1993, between Senator Christopher Bond (R-MO) and Senator Robert Byrd (D-WV). The differences in the two senators' assessments of the effects of the economic and fiscal policies of the previous 12 years of Republican rule, and their projections of how the Clinton economic plan would affect the economy and the budget in the years ahead were like night and day. The following excerpts from the senators' remarks are reproduced from the Congressional Record.

Mr. BOND. Mr. President, this debate is about keeping faith with the American people. This debate is about ensuring that the Federal Government does not destroy our economy. We have heard today that the stock market took a heavy hit yesterday and was down, and that consumer confidence is down.

I think I can tell you the reason that confidence is down. I think I can tell you why the markets are saying we are not going to see profits, we are not going to see growth, we are not going to see jobs, because this body—appropriately enough on April Fools' Day—passed a budget resolution saying that we would increase taxes a whopping $273 billion. The tax rates that would be jacked up under that resolution may contend that they will raise $273 billion. But we have learned something about taxes, and that is that taxes discourage economic activity. . . .

. . . If you look at the economic game plan that President Clinton has asked for and that the majority in both Houses have adopted, the economic game plan is a recipe for disaster. This so-called stimulus package, which I think is more appropriately labeled an "emergency deficit increase package," is going in exactly the opposite direction of what is needed. . . .

. . . But with 273 billion dollars' worth of tax increases, the Clinton plan, endorsed by this body, turns back up again and by the year 2000 the deficit is back up to $300 billion a year. . . .

. . . Our leader, Senator Dole, with our Budget Committee leader, Senator Domenici, presented an alternative budget deficit reduction plan that would save more than the Clinton budget adopted by this body would save, and they did it without increasing taxes. . . .

. . . At some point, the government is not going to be able to finance its debt. We are essentially going to be bankrupt.

But, in any event, we are going to be putting a tremendous burden on our children and our children's children. They are going to have to pay taxes on that. They are not going to enjoy the standard of living we have, or certainly the standard of living we would like to see them have, because our increased taxes in the budget resolution—the increases in spending there, plus the increased spending that is proposed in this package before us—will go on to their credit cards. And that is a dirty trick.

I see many young people coming to Washington, full of hope, full of optimism. I am embarrassed to tell them that we have already put $4 trillion of debt on their credit cards.

And during the first—and I trust the only—Clinton administration, we would add another $1.25 trillion to that debt.

The Republican members of this body are united. We have fought to bring some economic sense out of our current budget. We have said: "Cut the additional spending. Don't jack up taxes, particularly when they are going to kill jobs."

. . . We talk about 7 percent unemployment. I believe that the taxes in this measure will drive that unemployment figure even higher, and thus add to the deficit. Spending, if it is left unchecked, is going to drive the deficit back up even with taxes.

We believe the time has come to get serious about the deficit. And the only way to get serious is to cut spending. . . .

. . . The American people are tired of the politics of the past, where Congress continued to vote more and more money without regard to revenues. The tax-and-spend philosophy has not worked. We are attempting to keep faith with the American people who thought we would get a handle on spending.

If we spend money now, and more money that the government does not have, we will leave the bill for someone else down the road—and that is our children.

Mr. President, there is much more that could be said about this, but I know others want to speak."

Senator Bond painted a very scary picture of what would happen to the American economy and the federal budget if President Clinton's economic package was enacted into law, and he didn't even hint at a link between the Reagan tax cuts and the soaring budget deficits. Senator Byrd, however, saw both the past and the future through very different lenses. Excerpts from Senator Byrd's remarks follow.

Mr. BYRD. Mr. President, the distinguished senator said the time has come to get serious about the deficit.

Mr. President, let us go back over the past 12 years and talk about this deficit that the distinguished senator has said the time has come to get serious about.

Up until the first fiscal year for which Mr. Reagan was responsible, there had been no triple-digit billion-dollar deficit. Throughout the previous 39 administrations and the previous 192 years of history, this country had never run a triple-digit billion-dollar deficit.

We had gotten into some double-digit billion-dollar deficits under Mr. Ford, $70 billion, $50 billion the next year; under Mr. Carter, $55 billion, $38 billion, $73 billion, and $74 billion.

Then came the Reagan era. The first fiscal year for which Mr. Reagan was responsible, a $120 billion deficit. Never heard of before; unheard of before.

The next year, $208 billion; the next year, $186 billion; the next year, $222 billion; the next year; $238 billion; the next year, $169 billion; the next year, $194 billion; the next year, $250 billion; the next year, $278 billion.

That is the first fiscal year for which Mr. Bush was responsible. He had been trained very well under Mr. Reagan, his predecessor.

So in his first fiscal year for which he was responsible, a $278 billion deficit; the next year, $322 billion; the next year, $340 billion; and the next year, $352 billion.

Now, Mr. President, we hear all of this palavering about the deficit; the time has come to get serious about the deficit.

After all of this?

Our new president is trying to get serious. He has just been in office 73 days. He has sent up a package which is a well-balanced package. It is composed of three elements: deficit reduction, long-term investment in infrastructure, and short-term jobs investment. That is what the bill before the Senate does.

Now, the distinguished senator from Missouri says, and I am quoting him: "The tax-and-spend philosophy will not work."

Well, Mr. President, what I have just shown about this chart concerning the Federal deficits, fiscal years 1979-93—there are the deficits. We are told now that the tax and spend philosophy will not work. Under the Reagan administration, under the Bush administration, we were following a borrow and spend philosophy, a borrow and spend philosophy.

Mr. President, what happened to the total debt as a result of these deficits? When we run deficits, we increase the debt. We are talking about the last 12 years. We are not talking about the previous 192 years in this Republic's history, during which time the country ran up a total of $932 billion in debt; $932 billion. Less than $1 trillion. But because of the budgets that occurred during the Reagan and Bush years, the triple-digit billion-dollar deficits, we ran up a debt of $4,114 billion as of March 1, 1993.

So when the distinguished senator says he is embarrassed when schoolchildren ask him, why do we not do something? What is happening to our economy? He is embarrassed about the deficits; he is embarrassed about the debt; he is embarrassed about the interest on the debt. Mr. President, there it is. Under whose presidencies did that debt mushroom, like the prophet's gourd, overnight; from less than $1 trillion, from January 20, 1981, when President Reagan first took office, to $4,114 billion on March 1 of this year?

Tell the schoolchildren about that. Tell them when the deficits occurred. Tell them under whose administration those deficits occurred.

Mr. President, when those schoolchildren talk to the senator from Missouri he is going to tell them about the interest on that debt, and rightly so. But the interest on the debt when Mr. Reagan took office was $69 billion in that year. And in fiscal year 1993 it is $198.7 billion. Almost $199 billion. Almost $200 billion.

So, Mr. President, tell those children—I hope the Senator will not be embarrassed to tell them when those deficits occurred, when that debt quadrupled, and when the interest on the debt rose from $69 billion to almost $200 billion.

That is a hidden tax, $200 billion a year. That is a hidden tax, a hidden tax. And it is caused by those burgeoning deficits that took place over the last 12 years—a hidden tax.

This president is trying to do something about that hidden tax. He is trying to reduce the budget deficits and eventually, in time, to reduce the debt and concomitantly, the interest on the debt. So I just hope what I said will be helpful to the distinguished senator from Missouri when he faces those children who are—embarrassed about the deficits.

My grandchildren, my two daughters, and my two sons-in-law are embarrassed, too, about the debt. But I tell them how it arose. And the president, this president who has been in office just 73 days—73 days—is trying to do something about it. . . .

. . . Let this president have a chance. Give him a chance.

The Clinton economic plan, called the 1993 Budget Reconciliation Act, was passed without a single Republican vote in either the House or the Senate. Vice President Gore's tie-breaking vote was required to pass the measure in the Senate on August 6, 1993, and President Clinton signed the legislation into law four days later.

Passage of the Clinton economic plan marked a major historic turning point. It reversed 12 years of supply-side economics, more commonly known as Reaganomics. In addition, it committed the nation to a path of fiscal discipline that ultimately erased the massive budget deficits. With the benefit of hindsight, let's look at the economic record of the Clinton administration.

During the Clinton years, the nation experienced the longest economic expansion in American history. More than 22 million new jobs were created in less than 8 years, the most ever under a single administration. The unemployment rate dropped from 7 percent in 1993 when Clinton took office to 4 percent in November of 2000. The overall unemployment rate was the lowest in 30 years, and the unemployment rate for women fell to the lowest rate in 40 years.

In terms of the federal budget, the record $340.5 billion non-Social Security deficit in the last year of the Bush presidency was transformed into a record non-Social Security surplus of $86.6 billion in 2000.

The Republicans, who made it clear in 1993 that they did not want to be held responsible for the results of the Clinton economic package, began grasping for partisan explanations when the results turned out to be just the opposite of what they had predicted. Former Vice President Dan Quayle probably spoke for most Republicans when he said, "We do have prosperity, but let's give credit where credit is due. Ronald Reagan started the prosperity we have today. George Bush continued it, and Bill Clinton inherited it."

A close look at the record shows just how inaccurate Quayle's statement was. As stated in Chapter 4, President Reagan had the worst unemployment record of any modern president. During his first four-year term, the average annual unemployment rate was 8.6 percent—7.6 percent in 1981, 9.7 percent in 1982, 9.6 percent in 1983, and 7.5 percent in 1984. At no other time since the Great Depression of the 1930s had the unemployment rate ever been as high for a single year, let alone for a 4-year average. The average annual unemployment rate for Reagan's full 8-year presidency was 7.5 percent.

In terms of financial status, the national debt doubled from $1 trillion to $2 trillion during the first 6 years of the Reagan presidency. It was more than $2.6 trillion when Reagan left office, and it had soared above the $4 trillion mark by the time George Bush's 4-year presidency had ended.

Republicans have sought to deny President Clinton credit for the deficit reduction and the strong economy during the Clinton years. After all, they opposed his plan and did not contribute even one Republican vote, in either the House or the Senate, to its passage. Even worse, they were adamant in their predictions that the plan would devastate the economy and make the budget deficit worse.

However, numerous experts whose opinions were far more well-informed than those of partisan Republicans gave Clinton high marks on his economic and budgetary accomplishments. As early as the fall of 1994, former Federal Reserve Chairman, Paul Volcker, wrote, "The deficit has come down, and I give the Clinton administration and President Clinton himself a lot of credit for that . . . and I think we're seeing some benefits."

On February 20, 1996, Federal Reserve Chairman Alan Greenspan said the deficit reduction in the president's 1993 economic plan was "an unquestioned factor in contributing to the improvement in economic activity that occurred thereafter."

According to the June 17, 1996, issue of *U.S. News and World Report*, "President Clinton's budget deficit program begun in 1993 . . . [led] to lower interest rates, which begat greater investment growth (by double digits since 1993, the highest rate since the Kennedy administration), which begat 3-plus years of solid economic growth, averaging 2.6 percent annually, 50 percent higher than during the Bush presidency."

All the preceding comments came after only four years of the Clinton administration. Any remaining doubt about the positive results of the Clinton economic program should have been erased during the president's second term. The overall performance of the economy during Clinton's last four years in office was the best in the history of the nation.

Credit for the strong economy during the Clinton years, and for the transformation of the budget from massive deficits to the $86.6 billion surplus in 2000, should go largely to the highly talented economic advisers that Clinton surrounded himself with, and ultimately to Clinton himself for listening to their advice and acting accordingly.

Just before his inauguration, Clinton had held an economic summit in Little Rock, at which business executives, financiers, and academics, one after another, moaned about how huge federal borrowing to cover debt was making capital too expensive to allow industry to grow. He listened, and put together a team of top economic advisers to help him chart a new course. But even more important than Clinton's appointment of talented economic advisers, was his ability to understand the advice and implement much of it. Laura Tyson became chairperson of the Council of Economic Advisers. Bob Rubin, a widely respected financier, became secretary of the Treasury, and Harvard economist Lawrence Summers became undersecretary of the Treasury. All of these people argued that the economic health of the nation required major reductions in the deficit.

Of course, this was not a new argument. Harvard economist Martin Feldstein, who had served as Reagan's chairman of the Council of Economic Advisers, had made the same argument to Reagan and to the American people. Feldstein, however, soon learned that his advice was not going to be taken seriously because it was in conflict with the political objectives of the Reagan administration.

President George Herbert Walker Bush also was advised by his economic advisers to reduce the deficits. However, implementing the advice of his economic advisers was in conflict with Bush's political objectives, so he chose to ignore them. Both Reagan and George Bush gave their own political objectives a higher priority than sound economic policies. Most likely, on the day he was defeated in his bid for reelection by Bill Clinton, President George Bush wished he had paid more attention to his economic advisers.

In the February 2001 issue of *The Atlantic Monthly*, J. Bradford DeLong, an economist at the University of California at Berkeley, wrote the following about the difference between Bill Clinton and his predecessors when it came to listening to economic advisers.

> The difference between Bill Clinton and his predecessors lies not in the advice that he was given, but in the fact that he had the brains to understand it and the guts to follow through . . . Lifting the dead weight of the deficit from the economy cost him essentially all his political capital in 1993. And the rewards in terms of faster economic growth have been greater than anyone in 1993 would have dared predict . . . Economists will argue for decades to come over how much of the high-tech high-productivity growth boom we are currently experiencing is the result of the high-investment economy produced by the elimination of the deficit. It is a welcome change from the previous sport that academic economists played, that of assigning blame for relative stagnation.

Clinton's economic policies were based on the same traditional economic theory that had dominated American economic policy for more than 40 years prior to the election of President Reagan. That theory, usually referred to as Keynesian economics, has undergone substantial refinement and revision, but much of modern Keynesian economics is still rooted in the ideas set forth by Keynes.

Keynes argued that government should play an active role in maintaining the proper level of total spending in the economy in order to minimize both unemployment and inflation. He believed that with the proper use of the government's spending and taxing powers, the extremes of the business cycle could be avoided.

The size of the Gross Domestic Product (GDP), which is a measure of the total production of goods and services in the economy, is very important. So is the rate of growth of the GDP, because these two factors are the major determinants of the standard of living. If the GDP grows too slowly, or actually declines, there will be an increase in the number of people unemployed, whereas if it grows too rapidly, there may be an increase in inflation.

The level of total production, and thus the level of employment, in the American economy is determined by the level of total spending (aggregate demand) for goods and services. American producers will produce just about as much as they can profitably sell. If sales fall off and inventories start to build up, a producer will lay off workers and curtail production to whatever level can be sold profitably. When sales pick up again, and demand exceeds the current level of production, the producer will recall laid-off workers and expand production up to the point where production equals demand.

Thus, the key to a properly functioning economy is to maintain the proper level of total spending (aggregate demand), which is made up primarily of consumer spending, investment spending, and government spending. Through its spending and taxing powers, the government can have some control over the level of aggregate demand. If the economy is in a recession, with high unemployment, either increased government spending or increased consumer spending can help it to recover. A tax cut that puts additional take-home pay in the hands of consumers will almost certainly result in increased spending. However, it is especially important that the tax cut be temporary, and of the proper amount to stimulate the economy back to full employment without adding significantly to long-term deficits.

Most Keynesian economists believe that the government should aim for a roughly balanced budget over the long run. For example, over the course of the business cycle, the government's total spending should be approximately equal to its total revenue. During periods of recession and high unemployment, tax collections will decline and there will be an automatic increase in government spending for unemployment compensation and similar programs. However, as the economy recovers from the recession, and laid-off workers return to work, there will be increased tax revenue and a decline in spending for unemployment compensation and similar programs. If Keynesian economic policies are followed consistently, there will be deficits in some years and small surpluses in other years. It is to be hoped that, over a period of years, the two will roughly balance out.

In addition to the automatic changes in government spending and tax collections that occur over the course of the business cycle, most Keynesian economists believe that the government should use temporary tax cuts to stimulate the economy during periods of recession and rising unemployment. What Keynesian economists do *not* support is large structural changes in the tax system that will lead to large budget deficits for years to come.

Keynesian economists are deeply concerned about the effect that massive federal borrowing will have on interest rates. If businesses and consumers have to compete with the federal government for scarce funds, interest rates will inevitably rise. Higher interest rates discourage both business investment and consumer spending. Thus, ongoing large deficits alone can cause ongoing high unemployment.

President Clinton recognized the validity of Keynesian principles of economics, and he surrounded himself with competent economists who could advise him on proper government actions. The eight years of prosperity, and the transformation of massive deficits into a respectable surplus by 2000, were not accidental. The Clinton administration practiced sound economic policies, and the economy and the American people benefited enormously.

In short, both the budget and the economy were in great shape when Clinton turned over the reins of power to George W. Bush on

The gross domestic product (GDP) is a measure of the dollar value of the total production of goods and services in the economy in a year's time. The GDP tells policy makers how well the economy is doing. In a sense, GDP numbers are like the speedometer on a car. They tell us whether the economy is growing too fast, too slowly, or at the appropriate rate for sustained prosperity.

The size, and the rate of growth, of the GDP are very important because they are the major determinants of the standard of living. If the GDP grows too slowly, or actually declines, there will be an increase in the number of people unemployed, whereas, if it grows too rapidly, increased inflation may occur. The level of total spending (aggregate demand) in the economy is the primary determinant of the level of GDP.

In order to understand how the level of aggregate demand in the economy determines the level of GDP, it is helpful to look at how the level of total production is determined in a single factory. Suppose you own and operate a small manufacturing plant that produces quality bookcases. You have a number of distributors for your product and, for quite some time, you have been producing and selling approximately 500 bookcases per week. Since you know that the demand for your product can fluctuate up or down, you maintain an inventory of 400 bookcases in a warehouse.

If there should be a sudden increase in the demand from 500 to 600 bookcases per week, you could sell from your reserve inventory, as well as from current production, temporarily. However, the warehouse reserves will last for only four weeks. Therefore, you will probably hire additional workers and increase current production to 600 bookcases per week if the demand remains at that level for very long.

Now suppose that just the opposite occurs. After being able to sell 500 bookcases per week for more than a year, sales suddenly begin to decline and demand soon falls to only 400 bookcases per week. You will not continue to produce 500 bookcases per week, indefinitely, if you are able to sell only 400 per week. As unpleasant as it may be, you will need to consider laying off some of your workers and reducing production to 400 bookcases per week so that production will again be in balance with sales. In summary, the number of bookcases you will produce per week will be determined by the number you can sell. If customers increase their purchases of bookcases, you will increase production. But, if they reduce purchases, you will reduce production accordingly. Over the long run, you will produce just about as many bookcases as you can sell.

What is true for an individual factory is true for the economy as a whole. Just as you will increase or decrease production, and the size of your workforce, depending on the level of sales, the economy as a whole will adjust production, and the number of workers employed, when the level of total spending (aggregate demand) rises or falls. In other words, if total spending in the economy increases, total production (GDP), and the number of workers employed, will also rise. On the other hand, if total spending decreases, total production (GDP) and employment will decline.

Therefore, during a recession, the only way to increase the GDP, and thus employment, is to increase one or more of the three basic components of aggregated demand. The three basic components of aggregate demand are: (1) consumer spending, (2) business investment spending on new plant and equipment, and (3) government spending. Since we should never increase government spending just for the sake of stimulating the economy, and since business investment spending will increase in response to an increase in consumer spending, the primary focus of any attempt to stimulate the economy should be on getting consumers to spend more.

Consumer spending is determined by the level of consumer confidence and by the amount of income that consumers have. The amount of control that the government has over consumer confidence is very limited. However, through tax policy, the government can temporarily increase the amount of income that consumers have. Any tax cut designed to stimulate the economy and reduce unemployment must be targeted primarily at those consumers who will spend the additional income.

January 20, 2001. Bush chose to return to the failed economic policies of his father and Ronald Reagan, policies that have very little support among professional economists. America is already paying a high price for that mistake and the long term costs of Bush's actions are immeasurable.

Despite his positive contributions to the economy and the federal budget, President Clinton must be faulted for the role he played in deceiving the American public about the true status of the federal budget. Like both George Bush who preceded him, and George W. Bush, his successor, Clinton continued to use the surplus in the Social Security fund to understate the true deficits in the government operating budget, and once the budget was balanced and we experienced two years of surpluses, he used the same accounting procedures to overstate the size of the surpluses.

Bill Clinton was the one who gave birth to the budget-surplus myth. He is the one who first proclaimed the "good news" that the federal government had excess money. It was on Clinton's watch that the Social Security trust fund surplus first became large enough to more than offset the continuing on-budget deficit. It was President Clinton who announced a $69.2 billion federal budget surplus in 1998 when there was really a $30 billion on-budget deficit. It was Clinton who told the American people that the nation ran a $124.4 billion surplus in 1999 when every dollar of it except for the $1.9 billion real surplus, was in the Social Security trust fund, earmarked for funding the retirement of the baby boomers.

To be specific, in 1998, Clinton simply took the $99.2 billion Social Security surplus for that year, and subtracted the on-budget deficit of $30 billion to arrive at the mythical figure of a $69.2 billion surplus. In fiscal 1999, the government experienced a *real* on-budget (operating) surplus of $1.9 billion, the first federal surplus in almost 40 years. However Clinton was not content to just report the real surplus to the public. Instead, he added the $123.7 billion Social Security surplus for 1999 to the $1.9 billion real surplus and reported the combined total to the American public as the actual surplus.

Finally, in fiscal 2000, there was an unprecedented non-Social Security surplus of $86.6 billion. This was really something for Clinton to crow about, but instead of reporting the actual non-Social Security surplus, Clinton added the $149.8 billion Social Security surplus and reported a surplus of more than $230 billion. If he had just been honest with the public, Clinton's true record of deficit reduction would have been phenomenal. The Budget Enforcement Act of 1990 prohibited Clinton from combining the Social Security and non-Social Security budgets for purposes of reporting deficits or surpluses. But he chose to deceive the American people about the true status of the budget.

It would have been bad enough if this had been the extent of Clinton's accounting mischief. But it was only the beginning. He claimed that the budget surpluses would continue for as far as the eye could see. On June 26, 2000, President Clinton announced that over the next decade, the federal budget surplus would total nearly $1.9 trillion. This outrageous deliberate lie to the American people was the greatest sin of the Clinton presidency. It dwarfed the alleged misconduct that ultimately led to his impeachment.

From that point on, the American people seemed to believe that there truly was excess money in the federal budget, and cunning politicians began building schemes to further mislead the public into believing that surplus money was available for new programs and/or for tax cuts. Clinton had given birth to a monster in the form of the budget-surplus myth; it would later enable George W. Bush to get by with reckless actions that would threaten America's economic and budgetary future.

How could the president of the United States make such reckless claims? How could the American people be so gullible? The $1.9 trillion projected ten-year surplus that Clinton announced on June 26, 2000, was more than 2½ times what the administration had predicted it would be just three months earlier in February! How could anyone give any credibility to a procedure that yielded a projection 2½ times higher than it had been such a short while earlier?

Clinton did signal the dubious nature of this projection by raising the following red flag:

> This is just a budget projection. It would not be prudent to commit every penny of a future surplus that is just a projection and therefore subject to change."
> It would be a big mistake to commit this entire surplus to spending or tax cuts . . . The projections could be wrong, they could be right.

President Clinton did the country a great disservice with that announcement. He knew how it would be interpreted by the media, and his motives for making it were exclusively political. After eight years of dealing with budget figures, he had to have known that the projections were definitely wrong. He also knew that whatever the size of any budget surpluses over the next decade, most, if not all, of the money would belong to the Social Security trust fund.

Clinton's political motives for making the announcement were twofold. First of all, he wanted to exaggerate just how much the budget picture had improved under his presidency. Second, he probably thought the announcement would help Vice President Gore's campaign.

Strangely enough, the announcement probably helped George W. Bush far more than it helped Gore. The cornerstone of Bush's campaign was his proposed large tax cut, and he needed evidence that the cut was affordable. The Bush camp released the following statement in reaction to Clinton's announcement.

> Today's report confirms the accuracy of the conservative estimates Governor Bush used in preparing his balanced budget plan. The report also demonstrates the importance of passing the governor's tax cuts to prevent all this new money from being spent on bigger government.

It is hard to know whether Bush really believed there was any surplus money or not, but it is highly unlikely that he thought there would be the kind of future surpluses that Clinton had announced.

With all the publicity about the misuse of Social Security funds by his father, George W. Bush had to be aware that most of the surplus money was Social Security money, specifically earmarked for funding the post-2010 surge in retirement.

Surely Bush was aware that the United States government had more than $4.5 trillion in unpaid bills just from the previous twenty years of deficit spending. The younger Bush should also have known that his father's administration had spent $1.1 trillion more than it collected in revenue during President George Bush's four-year term.

George W. Bush should have been trying to find ways to undo the damage done during the Reagan-Bush years by paying down at least part of the debt accumulated during those years of irresponsible deficit spending. He had to know that cutting taxes was just about the worst thing the government could do at that point. But cutting taxes had gotten Reagan to the White House, and that's where George W. Bush intended to go.

Equally irresponsible were the statements of Vice President Gore. It is easy to understand Gore's motivation. Like George W. Bush, he was trying to ride the budget-surplus myth right into the White House. Gore felt that he had to promise increased spending on domestic programs to get elected, just as Governor Bush believed that his promised tax cuts would get *him* elected. Both were citing the mythical budget surplus as the source of funds to pay for their promises.

It is hard to understand why President Clinton behaved so irresponsibly with regard to the budget-surplus myth. Despite the many personal shortcomings of his presidency, I do believe that historians will record that President Clinton pursued sound economic and budgetary policies throughout most of his presidency that left the economy and the federal budget in much better shape when he left office than when he began his presidency. He did, however, create and feed the myth that the government had excess money when he should have been urging caution and pointing out that there was no surplus money with which to finance either Al Gore's promises or George W. Bush's proposed tax cut.

CHAPTER SIX

George W. Bush

Another Round of Reaganomics

~

My plan pays down an unprecedented amount of our national debt. And then, when money is still left over, my plan returns it to the people who earned it in the first place . . . My budget protects all $2.6 trillion of the Social Security surplus for Social Security, and for Social Security alone . . . We owe it to our children and grandchildren to act now, and I hope you will join me to pay down $2 trillion in debt during the next 10 years . . . That is more debt, repaid more quickly than has ever been repaid by any nation at any time in history.

—George W. Bush, [February 27, 2001]

O N FEBRUARY 27, 2001, President George W. Bush delivered his first State of The Union address to a joint session of Congress and to the American people. In this speech, he laid the foundation for his plan to enact massive tax cuts that would benefit primarily the wealthiest 5 percent of Americans. He also skillfully pulled the wool over the eyes of the public through a series of deceptive statements designed to convince Congress that the coffers of the United States government were overflowing with billions of surplus dollars for as far as the eye could see. "Deceptive statements" is putting it mildly; to put it more bluntly, he lied to the American people about the financial status of the federal budget.

The following are excerpts from the speech.

Our new governing vision says government should be active, but limited; engaged, but not overbearing. And my budget is based on that philosophy. It is reasonable, and it is responsible. . . . My plan pays down an unprecedented amount of our national debt. And then, when money is still left over, my plan returns it to the people who earned it in the first place.

. . . To make sure the retirement savings of America's seniors are not diverted in any other program, my budget protects all $2.6 trillion of the Social Security surplus for Social Security, and for Social Security alone.

. . . My budget has funded a responsible increase in our ongoing operations. It has funded our nation's important priorities, it has protected Social Security and Medicare. And our surpluses are big enough that there is still money left over.

Many of you have talked about the need to pay down our national debt. I listened and I agree. We owe it to our children and grandchildren to act now, and I hope you will join me to pay down $2 trillion in debt during the next 10 years . . . That is more debt, repaid more quickly than has ever been repaid by any nation at any time in history.

We should also prepare for the unexpected, for the uncertainties of the future. We should approach our nation's budget as any prudent family would, with a contingency fund for emergencies or additional spending needs. For example, after a strategic review, we may need to increase defense spending. We may need to increase spending for our farmers or additional money to reform Medicare. And so, my budget sets aside almost a trillion dollars over 10 years for additional needs. That is one trillion additional reasons you can feel comfortable supporting this budget.

We have increased our budget at a responsible 4 percent. We have funded our priorities. We paid down all the available debt. We have prepared for contingencies. And we still have money left over.

. . . Now we come to a fork in the road; we have two choices. . . . We could spend the money on more and bigger government. That's the road our nation has traveled in recent years.

. . . If you continue on that road, you will spend the surplus and have to dip into Social Security to pay other bills. Unrestrained government spending is a dangerous road to deficits, so we must take a different path. The other choice is to let the American people spend their own money to meet their own needs.

I hope you will join me in standing firmly on the side of the people. You see, the growing surplus exists because taxes are too high and government is charging more than it needs. The people of America have been overcharged and, on their behalf, I am here asking for a refund.

Perhaps never before in history had the American people been played for such fools by their president. Most people know very little about such things as economics and the federal budget, so they must trust someone to tell them the truth. Surely they could trust a new president who was asking for their support to be straightforward with them. If he said the government had trillions of dollars of surplus money, it must be true, regardless of how implausible it seemed. And he wasn't the only top official to say so. Both President Clinton and Vice President Gore had spoken of large surpluses.

But of course, there was the disturbing fact that many economists were saying there was no surplus. On September 27, 2000, exactly five short months prior to the President's address, I appeared on CNN TODAY with Lou Waters to discuss my newly published book, *The Alleged Budget Surplus, Social Security, and Voodoo Economics*. Its basic theme was that there *was* no true surplus. I argued that the government had been lying to the American people for several years about the real status of the federal budget and the Social Security trust fund. I pointed out that there was not a single dollar of reserves in the Social Security trust fund, because the government had been borrowing from the fund for several years and using the money to fund other programs.

Excerpts follow from the transcript of my interview with Lou Waters on CNN.

CNN Today

Economist Allen Smith Discusses *The Alleged Budget Surplus, Social Security & Voodoo Economics*

Aired September 27, 2000 - 2:01 p.m. ET

LOU WATERS, CNN Anchor: You know that old song "We're in the Money"? You might hear a few Washington politicians humming that tune today. Thanks to a well-greased economic machine that, like that battery-powered bunny, just keeps on ticking.

The federal government is ending the fiscal year this week flush with cash, apparently, $230 billion in surplus, the largest surplus in U.S. history. President Clinton did a little election-year crowing, mentioning Al Gore by name at least twice as he ran down the numbers. Mr. Clinton says $223 billion of the surplus went toward the national debt, and he says there's something in that for you. Like we said, it's an election year.

(BEGIN VIDEO CLIP)

WILLIAM J. CLINTON, President of the United States: Paying off the debt will benefit America just as paying off credit cards benefits the average family. It frees up money for things that matter and it keeps interest rates lower. That will mean more investment, more jobs, lower mortgage payments, car payments and student loan payments.

(END VIDEO CLIP)

WATERS: Washington posted its first surplus since the Vietnam War era. In 1998, $69 billion; almost double the next year to $124 billion; and now, in 2000, the surplus has just about doubled again to $230 billion.

The person you're about to meet might accuse the federal government of economic malpractice. He is economist Allen Smith, who says there is no surplus, that it's all a big, fat myth. His book is entitled *The Alleged Budget Surplus, Social Security & Voodoo Economics.*

Dr. Smith joins us from Ft. Myers, Florida. He taught economics for 30 years, retiring from Eastern Illinois University in 1998 to write. And he wrote this book entitled, once again, *The Alleged Budget Surplus, Social Security & Voodoo Economics,* all of which suggests you're not elated over President Clinton's announcement today of 19 billion more in the surplus since June.

ALLEN SMITH, Author, *The Alleged Budget Surplus, Social Security & Voodoo Economics:* The figures released today I haven't seen, the breakdown in terms of the amount that is off budget and the amount that is on budget. But like all the other surpluses they've been talking about, most of this is Social Security money and Social Security Trust Fund. Prior to the figures released today, in the last 40 years, we had a surplus in the operating budget of seven-tenths of a billion, or 700 million, and that came in fiscal '99. Thirty-eight years prior to that, every year had a deficit in operating budget. This is Social Security money they're talking about and not general tax revenue.

WATERS: You're saying that this money that we're hearing is a government surplus that we're paying down the federal debt with is Social Security money?

SMITH: It is Social Security money and they are not paying down the national debt. If I could, I just went on the Internet to the Treasury Department's Web site and printed out—they have a page on there— the public debt to the penny. And they give it—they show a public debt of two years ago, in 1998, of 5,526 billion, and today it is 5,646. According to the Treasury Department official figures, the national debt has increased by $120 billion in this two-year period in which Clinton says it's being paid down.

What they're doing is borrowing from Social Security money, paying off what they describe as the publicly held debt and trying to make the American people believe the debt's going down.

WATERS: Well, if what you say is true, what do we make of these political promises of a prescription drug benefit, preschool for all, college tuition paid for, tax cuts? We heard Al Gore just a few minutes ago saying they, meaning Republicans, would squander the surpluses. And he's talking about a tax cut.

SMITH: These are outrageous proposals, both the proposals of George W. Bush and that of Al Gore, will tend to derail the economy, as has happened so many times before. I don't know if they've consulted with any economists, if they've looked at the facts. But Al Gore has said we'll be debt-free by 2012, and you can—anybody can go to the Internet and get this "Mid-Session Review." It's from the office of the president, the OMB, submitted to Congress in June. And the figures in here will show that President Clinton is showing an increase in the national debt between 2000 and 2012 of about close to an additional trillion dollars.

WATERS: So we're being misled by the politicians with all these campaign promises?

SMITH: We are being totally deceived. I think this is the biggest deception in American history. It started back about 10 years ago under President Bush at the time the Social Security surpluses first came into being.

I think what the American people need to know, and most don't seem to know, and I don't hear it anyplace in the news, is the so-called "surplus" all originated as a result of legislation passed in 1983 in reaction to a presidential commission headed by Alan Greenspan in 1982 which indicated we were going to have major problems with Social Security when the baby boomers retired, beginning about 2010.

So they took action, they raised tax rates and the sort. Every bit of this surplus is a planned surplus and it is in the Social Security trust fund. I don't know the figures today, but as of last year, the only surplus that was not in Social Security was seven-tenths of a billion, or 700 million. And we have spent $4,600 billion of red ink in the last 20 years.

WATERS: I would certainly agree with you we're not hearing any of this in the news. I'm involved in the news. Are you a voice crying in the wilderness? And if not, why haven't we seen a presidential candidate, any presidential candidate, talk about this?

SMITH: I think because—there's one of—there's only two explanations. One, they don't know the facts, they don't know anything. The other is, they're deliberately misleading the American people. And I think it's the latter. George W. Bush's early proposal for the massive tax cut, that was just an unthinkable—that's more Reaganomics. It's exactly the same thing Ronald Reagan said. And when Ronald Reagan came into office, we had accumulated $1 trillion in debt. We now have 5.6 trillion; 4.6 trillion of that, or 82 percent, has come under Clinton, Bush and Reagan. And the American people seem to be of the impression that we don't have a debt because of the lack of a current deficit.

WATERS: I can hear boomers now. There are between 70 and 80 million of them saying if the Social Security surplus is being used to pay down the debt, what about my Social Security?

SMITH: Well, not only that, the Social Security money has all been used for general operating purposes since it first came out back in the early—or the late '80s. President Bush, at the time he was in office, he said, "read my lips: no new taxes," and yet he spent a substantial amount of the increased revenue from Social Security, the surplus that came along. Sen. Daniel Moynihan, at that time, actually suggested that we repeal that Social Security tax increase to keep them from getting it.

So we started back in the Bush administration pulling the wool over the American people's eyes, and it's been going on ever since.

WATERS: Is there a danger for the future?

SMITH: There is a big danger because our economy right now is healthy, extremely healthy, but the budget of the United States government is probably the worst it's ever been in terms of indebtedness, and any action taken by the government does have an impact on the economy. And I think that either—the plans of either of the two candidates will derail this economy and put us back into recession and major problems.

WATERS: But we all thought, because of the economy, because of more jobs, because of more people working and paying taxes and corporate profits up, corporate taxes up, that that's the reason why we have these surpluses.

SMITH: No.

WATERS: No.

SMITH: That is—the reason is the result of the 1983 tax increase. It is the reason that we had the tiny surplus last year. And probably, of the amount announced today, when they release the figures, they'll tell us how much of that 230 billion is in the Social Security fund and how much is in the general operating budget. My guess is there's not more than 30 billion there.

And we would expect that to be the case when the economy's at a point with the lowest unemployment in 30 years, but it won't continue. Recessions always follow expansions and we will be back in deficit territory before very long whether we have any tax cuts or not. And the tax cuts will just make it worse.

WATERS: A dire warning from economist Allen Smith. Thank you, Professor, for joining us today.

SMITH: Thank you for having me.

WATERS: The book: *The Alleged Budget Surplus, Social Security & Voodoo Economics.*

I was only one of many economists trying to alert the public to the "budget-surplus myth," months before President George W. Bush was even elected. Once Bush's election was certain, many economists tried to warn the public that his massive proposed tax cut would be disastrous for both the budget and the economy. But nobody wanted to listen to professional economists when their president was insisting that there was surplus money, and promising to give some of it back to them.

At the time of Bush's State of the Union address, the United States government owed approximately $5 trillion dollars more than it had owed just 20 years earlier when President Reagan had taken office. This represented $5 trillion of unpaid bills. Bush's own father had contributed greatly to this massive red-ink spending. During George H.W. Bush's four years as president, the on-budget deficit (excluding Social Security funds) averaged more than $286 billion per year. And when he left office, the national debt that had been only $1 trillion at the beginning of the Reagan-Bush administration had soared above the $4 trillion mark!

President Clinton also ran on-budget deficits during the first six years of his presidency. However, because of the Clinton deficit-reduction package, the deficits declined significantly during each of Clinton's first six years. Finally, in 1999, the deficit was totally eliminated, and there was a tiny surplus of $1.9 billion. In fiscal 2000, the federal budget had a surplus of $86.6 billion. These were the only two non-Social Security surpluses during the preceding 40-year period, and they may well prove to be the only two surpluses that many Americans will see during their entire lifetimes.

The budget returned to deficit territory during George W. Bush's first year in office, posting an on-budget deficit of $33.5 billion in fiscal 2001. The deficit soared to $317.5 billion in 2002, and to a projected record $467.6 billion for 2003. After that, the deficit is projected to be in the neighborhood of $500 billion per year for several years. Thus, instead of paying down the debt as promised, President Bush will be adding approximately as much to the debt in 2 years as was added during the first 200 years of American history!

George W. Bush should have been in a better position than almost anyone else to know just how dire the federal budget situation was and what a dismal failure Reaganomics had been during the 12 years Reagan and Bush were in office. His father was vice president for eight years under Reagan, and served four years as president. As the son of the vice president for eight years, and as the son of the president of the United States for four years, George W. Bush had access to information not available to many.

With aspirations to be president himself someday, the younger Bush must have talked shop with his father and tried to learn as much about the job as possible. Certainly he had to know that during those 12 years of Reagan and Bush, the national debt had quadrupled. Didn't he have any concern that Ronald Reagan and the elder Bush had added three times as much to the national debt in just 12 years as all the previous presidents in American history had added in nearly 200 years?

He must have shared his father's pain when the elder Bush failed to win reelection. And all he had to do to learn why his father had been defeated was listen to the news. It was the economy and the massive deficits that did his father in, just as it was Clinton's promise to reduce the deficits that brought victory to him. Knowing about those massive deficits during the Reagan-Bush years, and knowing how much the national debt had risen in just a few years, how could George W. Bush tell the American people that the government had surplus money?

There was no surplus money except for the Social Security fund, and Bush pledged not to touch that money. As for the surpluses in 1999 and 2000, during the Clinton administration, they weren't enough to even offset the 1997 deficit of $103.4 billion, let alone the other Clinton deficits. The surpluses of 1999 and 2000 came at the peak of the business cycle when the economy was in overdrive and the unemployment rate was at a 30-year low. Only under such conditions did the economy have the potential to generate enough revenue to even balance the budget. And let's remember that those two years were preceded by 38 consecutive years of deficits.

There was no way that there could be ongoing surpluses in the non-Social Security budget, as President George W. Bush learned when he ran a budget deficit during his very first year in office. The tax structure was barely capable of generating enough revenue to balance the budget in the top phase of the business cycle, when all resources were employed and the economy was producing at its maximum capacity. Only rarely, and for short periods of time, is the economy at this stage. At all other times, the economy is either in recession or in the process of recovering from a recession. During such times, the economy is not operating at the full-employment level, and experience over the previous 40 years had shown that in most years there would be at least a small deficit.

Despite these facts, President Bush told the nation that the government had massive surpluses. He did not use qualifying words such as "projected surplus" or "anticipated surplus." He talks of the surplus as if he already had it locked in a vault. Consider the following statement:

> We have increased our budget at a responsible 4 percent. We have funded our priorities. We paid down all the available debt. We have prepared for contingencies. And we still have money left over.

George W. Bush was talking about make-believe money, but he led his audience to believe that it was the real thing. He and his staff had manipulated the numbers in such a way as to create make-believe surpluses.

At the time of his first State of the Union address, Bush had not yet achieved any of the things he refers to; he has not achieved any of them since, and it would be absolutely impossible for him to achieve any of them in the future, given the fact that he is now rapidly leading the nation toward bankruptcy. These statements in his 2001 State of the Union address were lies designed to deceive and confuse the American people so they would support his call for massive tax cuts for the very rich.

He explains the reason for the nonexistent surplus as follows:

> The growing surplus exists because taxes are too high and government is charging more than it needs. The people of America have been over-charged and, on their behalf, I am here asking for a refund."

There was no growing surplus, except for the temporary, planned surplus in the Social Security trust fund. The non-Social Security budget had run deficits in 38 of the past 40 years. How could he say that the government was charging more in taxes than it needed when his own father had run an average non-Social Security deficit of more than $286 billion per year during his four years as president, and President Clinton had run deficits during six of his eight years as president?

As this book goes to press, there is a worldwide public furor over whether President George W. Bush deliberately misled the public in his 2003 State of the Union address by including a sentence about Iraq attempting to buy uranium from Africa. The statement turned out to be unsubstantiated by the CIA. Furthermore, the CIA had requested that a similar sentence be removed from a speech that Bush delivered in Cincinnati three months earlier and it rejected an earlier version of the sentence used in the State of the Union address. The sentence was reworded in an effort to overcome the objections of the CIA and was included in the 2003 address. Critics accused the President of being so eager to wage war against Iraq that he deliberately added the reference to frighten the nation's citizens over a possible nuclear attack on the United States by Iraq so they would be more supportive of a war.

Regardless of the outcome of the controversy over the 2003 State of the Union address, there is no question that President George W. Bush deliberately lied to the people in his 2001 State of the Union address. He did so in order to pass a massive tax cut that he knew was not in the best interest of the nation or the economy. It was political payback time. Those wealthy supporters who had given so much money to Bush's campaign had to be repaid; otherwise they might not be so generous when he ran for a second term.

In addition to misrepresenting the financial status of the federal budget, Bush also misrepresented the potential economic effects of his proposed tax cut. On February 8, 2001, in an effort to stampede his tax cut through Congress, Bush suggested that the economy was headed for trouble which his tax cut could prevent. Speaking at a Rose Garden ceremony, Bush said, "A warning light is flashing on the dashboard of our economy. And we can't just drive on and hope for the best. We must act without delay." The president said his 10-year, $1.6 trillion proposal would "jump-start the economy," and he argued that swift passage of his plan by Congress could make the difference between growth and recession.

Many observers were shocked that a new president who had been in office less than three weeks would make such an irresponsible statement and risk spooking the markets and lowering consumer confidence. When Franklin D. Roosevelt became president during the depth of the Great Depression, he said, "The only thing we have to fear is fear itself," in an effort to calm the public and build optimism. The fields of economics and psychology are so interwoven that if enough Americans come to believe that the nation is about to enter a recession, their behavior will actually cause one. People will respond to their fears by cutting back on spending in preparation for anticipated layoffs, and as new orders to factories begin to decline, workers will *indeed* be laid off.

To use such scare tactics to get a tax cut, which does little to stimulate the economy, is inexcusable for any president. Some observers suggested that Bush had another reason for making the statement. After the longest economic expansion in American history, during the Clinton presidency, it seemed almost a certainty that a recession would occur some time during President Bush's four years in office. Some accused him of trying to speed up the recession so that the economy would have gone through the recession and recovered by the time he had to run for a second term. No matter what his motives, there is little question that Bush's reckless statement did contribute, at least in a small way, to the recession that sent unemployment rates soaring to 6.4 percent by 2003.

The other flaw in his argument was that quick passage of his tax cut would stimulate the economy. Bush's original tax-cut proposal would have done little to provide short-term stimulus. It would have provided only $60 in tax relief during the first year for a single earner making $32,000, and only $120 during the first year for a married couple with a $57,000 income. To stimulate the economy in the short term, you must put money into the hands of those consumers who will spend it. Tax cuts for the wealthy result in little or no new consumer spending, because they already have sufficient purchasing power to buy whatever they need.

On the other hand, low-income consumers have many unmet needs, and will likely spend nearly all of any tax rebate they might receive. The $1.35 trillion tax cut bill that ultimately passed on May 26, 2001, did contain some stimulus in the form of tax rebates. These were added by Democrats in Congress who refused to vote for Bush's bill unless there was a provision for such rebates.

Despite Bush's continuing claims that there was plenty of non-Social Security surplus to fund his tax cuts, and despite his pledge not to use any of the Social Security surplus for anything but Social Security, when the numbers were in for fiscal 2001, the government ran a $33.4 billion deficit. The surplus of $86.6 billion during the last year of the Clinton presidency would be the last surplus for a very long time, if not forever.

This first year's record of Bush's economic and budgetary policies is very significant, because it was not in any way related to the terrorist attack or the resulting wars against terrorism and Iraq. Fiscal year 2001 ended on September 30, just 19 days after the September 11 attacks, so there was not enough time for any effects to be reflected in that year's budget.

It was also very difficult for Bush to blame that first deficit on a slowing economy. It had only been six months since his March 27 speech at Western Michigan University in which he said that his budget allowed for a "softening" economy.

> Tax relief is central to my plan to encourage economic growth, and we can proceed with tax relief without fear of budget deficits, even if the economy softens. Projections for the surplus in my budget are cautious and conservative. They already assume an economic slowdown in the year 2001.

Obviously Bush's budget calculations were way off the mark, either by design, or due to sloppy accounting procedures. As a result, George W. Bush began reaching into the Social Security cookie jar just seven months after he had solemnly uttered the following words in his State of the Union address:

> . . . To make sure the retirement savings of America's seniors are not diverted in any other program, my budget protects all $2.6 trillion of the Social Security surplus for Social Security, and for Social Security alone.

The Social Security trust fund was raided during Bush's very first year in office. I think there is little doubt that Bush knew he would be dipping into Social Security before the end of his term, but even he may have been surprised that the need came so soon.

It had been only four months since the $1.35 trillion, ten-year tax cut had been enacted into law with the assurances of the Bush administration that huge surpluses lay ahead. In April 2001, the White

House projected a surplus of $281 billion for the fiscal year. This projection included both the (off-budget) Social Security surplus, and the on-budget (operating budget) surplus, despite the fact that federal law prohibits including Social Security into the calculation of either deficits or surpluses.

When the final numbers were in, the non-Social Security budget recorded a deficit of $33.4 billion. Since this $33.4 billion deficit in the operating budget had to be borrowed from the planned, temporary Social Security surplus of $160.7 billion, the overall surplus, including Social Security, had dwindled from the April projection of $281 billion to only $127 billion in less than six months.

How could a budget projection be off by $154 billion less than six months before the end of the budget year? It couldn't! The figures that Bush used in April and May to arm-twist his tax cut through Congress had to be phony figures, and the administration had to know they were phony.

By early 2003, it was quite clear just how wrong Bush had been. The non-Social Security deficit for fiscal 2002 had been a whopping $317.5 billion, and a $467.6 billion deficit was being projected for fiscal 2003. The economy had stalled, the unemployment rate had risen to 6 percent, and 2 million jobs had been lost just since Bush took office. Obviously the huge $1.35 trillion tax cut had affected the economy very differently than Bush had predicted. So what kind of medicine did the economy need in 2003? According to Bush, we needed still more tax cuts, so in early 2003 he called for a large new tax-cut package, including elimination of the tax on dividend income.

When more than 400 of the nation's top economists placed a full-page ad in the *New York Times* to warn the public about the dangers of such action, President Bush, who had revealed his lack of understanding of even the most basic fundamentals of economics over and over during his speeches, totally ignored their warnings and campaigned against them and anyone else who opposed his latest tax cut. He also traveled around the country trying to convince the American public to put pressure on Congress to pass his proposal.

In the years to come, historians will almost certainly have difficulty explaining the action of the Senate on Friday, May 23, 2003. On that date, the Senate voted to raise the nation's debt limit by nearly $1 trillion, less than a week before the Treasury Department was expected to run out of borrowing authority and risk default on the nation's debt. There was nothing extraordinary about this in and of itself. Congress has been playing the game of putting a meaningless limit on how much the government can legally borrow for decades, but it always raises the limit whenever the government is about to exceed it. When Reagan took office, the legal limit on the national debt was less than $1 trillion, but it was systematically raised to accommodate the soaring debt that had exceeded the $4 trillion mark by the end of the Reagan-Bush administrations.

What was so extraordinary about the May 23, 2003, vote to raise the debt ceiling was the fact that it came on the very same day that the Senate also passed a $350 billion tax cut. If the financial condition of the United States government was so dire as to require almost a trillion-dollar increase in the debt ceiling, how in the world could a single senator justify voting for a $350 billion tax cut? The notion of financing a tax cut with borrowed money at a time when the national debt has risen by more than $5.5 trillion just since President Reagan took office is so radical and so irresponsible, it causes one to wonder if the members of Congress who voted for it had a good grasp of just how precarious the federal budget situation is. If they did understand what they were doing, then they put their own personal political interests above the interests of the nation and the American people.

The U.S. House of Representatives, in which the Republicans hold a much larger majority than in the Senate, passed the bill by a 231 to 200 margin. But the Senate ended up with a 50-50 tie vote. It took Vice President Cheney's tie-breaking vote to pass the bill in the Senate.

It is ironic that President Clinton's deficit-reduction package passed the Senate only by the tie-breaking vote of Vice President Al Gore. After so much damage to the budget by the Reagan tax cuts, Clinton eliminated the massive deficits in just six years. Now, by the same tie-breaking vote of the Republican Vice President, we are send-ing the budget back into massive deficit territory.

The tax cut of 2003 was the second Trojan horse that President Bush had given to the American public. His 2001 tax-cut package was based on the myth that the federal government had huge budget sur-pluses with which to pay for the tax cuts. He promised that his 2001 cuts would not bring a return of deficits and that Social Security money would not be used to pay for them. Since Bush had already been proven wrong about the surplus, the return to deficits, and the borrowing of Social Security surpluses, by 2003, he could no longer use that argument. Instead, in 2003, he pushed through a tax cut pri-marily benefiting the wealthy, masquerading as a "jobs-creation" bill.

A one-time tax rebate to people who would spend it on consumer goods could certainly have created many jobs at only a tiny fraction of the cost of the Bush plan, but the Bush plan was structured to give tax relief mostly to those in the high-income brackets, which would not stimulate much additional consumer spending. Bush knew that the economists were right and that his plan would not create many jobs, but he misled the public into believing that it was really a job-creation plan.

Did President Bush deliberately and knowingly lie to the Ameri-can people in order to facilitate political goals that were dear to him? This is a very touchy question. Many people believe that out of respect for the office of the presidency, we should not accuse a sitting presi-dent of lying, no matter how obvious it may seem.

Did President George W. Bush lie to the Congress and to the American public about the true financial condition of federal finances in order to get his tax cut through Congress? You decide. There is only one other possible explanation for what happened. That is, that the President did not have a clue about what was going on with the fed-eral budget; that he was deceived by his own advisers into believing that there would be non-Social Security surpluses, when in fact mas-sive deficits lay ahead for as far as the eye could see.

Take your pick. Either we have an economically illiterate president who can easily be duped about economic matters by his advisers, or we have a president who knowingly and deliberately lied to Congress and the American public about the financial status of the federal government in order to get his tax cut passed. Neither explanation gives me any comfort whatsoever.

I don't subscribe to the theory that it is wrong to accuse the president of lying when it is clear that he has lied, and obviously many members of Congress don't subscribe to it either. After all, what were the grounds for impeaching President Bill Clinton? They weren't his actions or his immorality. He was accused of lying in response to a question about his alleged affair with Monica Lewinsky. Now, President Clinton is only the second president in the history of this great nation to be impeached, and he was impeached for allegedly telling a lie.

It seems to me that Clinton's impeachment should send a loud and clear message to all presidents and other government officials. THOU SHALT NOT LIE! But if we were to remove from office all public officials who have lied to their constituents, would there be anyone left to run the government?

I suppose some would try to argue that Clinton's alleged lie was especially bad because he was under oath at the time. Well, correct me if I am wrong, but I seem to remember George W. Bush placing his hand on a Bible and taking an oath to uphold the Constitution and honorably discharge his duties as President just like all other presidents before him. Doesn't that oath apply 24 hours a day, 7 days a week, until his term of office expires?

Of course, there are times when a president may be serving the best interests of the nation by lying, when the national security is at stake, for example. But I find it hard to justify lying to the American people about economic and fiscal matters, especially when the motivation for the large tax cut could well be a desire to pay back wealthy campaign contributors. The seriousness of the lie is greatly increased when it may result in long-term damage to the economy and the livelihoods of millions of Americans.

America cannot afford to allow this charade to continue anymore. The time for truth is at hand. The president and members of Congress from both political parties have a moral responsibility to acknowledge the true condition of the government's finances. The people must be told that, just during the past 22 years, the government has accumulated more than $5.6 trillion in unpaid bills, and it is spending approximately *$1 billion per day of taxpayers' money just to cover the interest cost of that debt*. The public is entitled to know that 1999 and 2000 are the only two years in the past 40 years in which the government did not have an on-budget deficit, and that the exception for these two years was due primarily to the fact that the unemployment rate was at a 30-year low. Politicians who consistently and deliberately risk the future of our children and grandchildren, as well as the future of America itself, in order to achieve short-term political advantage, are not worthy of the public trust.

CHAPTER SEVEN

Tax Cuts and Job Creation

~

... Regardless of how one views the specifics of the Bush plan, there is wide agreement that its purpose is a permanent change in the tax structure and not the creation of jobs and growth in the near-term ... Passing these tax cuts will worsen the long-term budget outlook, adding to the nation's projected chronic deficits ...

—Statement signed by nation's top economists
[The *New York Times*, February 11, 2003.]

*I*F YOU SAY SOMETHING that people want to believe often enough, they begin to believe it. For example, back during the days of the budget-surplus myth, the American people were told repeatedly that the government had huge amounts of surplus money. They were told by Bill Clinton, Al Gore, George W. Bush, and many members of Congress. Journalists just seemed to accept the myth as true so they passed the good news on to everyone who would listen. Almost everybody got into the act, and organizations began running ads lobbying for part of the loot.

The big debate during the 2000 presidential election campaign was how to spend the unexpected manna from heaven. Gore wanted to spend a good portion of it for improved education, health care, and other programs. George W. Bush wanted to give it back to the people in the form of big tax cuts. Hardly anyone was asking such questions as: Is the surplus real? How could it be real? Where did it come from? Why have we never experienced such a phenomenon before? The American people were like tiny children who wanted so much to believe that Santa Claus was going to bring them lots of goodies that they failed to question whether or not there really was a true surplus.

Today, of course, we know that there never was any significant true surplus except for the temporary, planned, earmarked surpluses in the Social Security program that resulted from the 1983 Social Security tax increase. The fact that there were non-Social Security surpluses in 1999 and 2000 for the first time in 40 years was remarkable, but they were not even large enough to offset the deficits of 1997 and 1998. A $317.5 billion deficit in 2002 and a projected $467.6 deficit for 2003 made it clear that the nation was again operating deep in deficit territory.

The budget surplus was a very big lie told by many people. Some of them may have been so poorly informed about the budget situation that they actually believed what they were saying, but not the top leadership.

Another lie is that tax cuts of any kind stimulate the economy and result in the creation of many jobs. Tax cuts that put money into the hands of consumers who are not buying because they are unemployed, or because they are on a very tight budget, can stimulate the economy and create jobs. Tax cuts that go to people who already have almost everything that money can buy will have little or no positive effect on the economy or job creation. They will, however, lead to large budget deficits and a soaring national debt.

When the economy is in a recession with high levels of unemployment, the most effective way of giving it a boost is to put money in the hands of consumers who make up two-thirds of the total demand in the economy. The simplest and most effective way to accomplish this goal is through temporary one-time tax rebates. For example, a check for $500 might be sent to each American taxpayer, most of whom would probably spend it. Since it is a one-time rebate, and tax rates remain unchanged, it would have a very limited effect on deficits over the long run, but it would give the economy a jump-start, which is all that is needed to stimulate it out of recession.

If the primary goal of the tax rebate is to improve the economy, and policy makers don't get all caught up in the politics of who should get how much in terms of fairness, a strong case can be made for targeting most of the tax rebate to those people in the lowest income brackets, who will spend almost 100 percent of it on consumer goods and services.

As consumer spending increases and new orders begin coming into factories, the employers will begin calling back laid-off workers so they can increase production. When the newly recalled workers begin getting paychecks again, they will increase their spending, causing still more unemployed workers to be recalled. This process can continue until the economy once again regains full employment. If the first tax rebate is not sufficient stimulus, then another rebate can be used to complete the job.

When consumer demand is high, employers hire additional workers in order to fill the demand. This is the way jobs get created. The Bush position, that you should give tax breaks to businesses so they will create jobs, is just plain wrong. No amount of tax relief for businesses will cause them to create jobs if they cannot sell their products. *Demand* is what creates jobs. If a company has such strong demand for its products that it is turning away customers for lack of inventory, you can be absolutely sure that it will expand its productive capacity to meet the demand, and not a penny of government tax relief is necessary for the company to do this.

Tax cuts for the wealthy may be good politics for a president who gets much of his financial support from them, but it is lousy economics. When they get a tax cut they just turn it over to their accountant with instructions to find a good place to invest it. One of those "good places to invest" is with the United States Treasury.

Because of the tax cuts during the Reagan administration, plus those under George W. Bush, the national debt has soared and is destined to grow even faster as a result of the huge deficits under Bush.

The government must constantly finance and refinance this huge debt by borrowing. Since the government has to finance its deficits no matter how high the interest rate, it will always be competing with businesses and consumers for funds. This competition tends to drive interest rates up over the long run.

What happens to a lot of the money that wealthy Americans receive in the form of big tax cuts is that they loan it right back to the government and earn interest on it by investing it in United States Treasury notes and bonds. Money that was coming in to the government in the form of tax revenue now comes in in the form of borrowed money on which interest must be paid. Tax cuts for high-income people play almost no role in the creation of new jobs, because for tax cuts to stimulate the economy and create jobs, they must result in new spending for goods and services.

The idea of cutting tax rates permanently at a time when tax revenue falls far short of expenditures is almost suicidal. It makes no economic sense whatsoever. When you jump start your car with another battery, once the engine starts, you remove the secondary battery. Jump starting the economy should work the same way. With a one-time jolt in the form of a tax rebate, the economy should take off on its own. If the first jolt is not sufficient to stimulate the economy back to the full-employment level, you might give it another jolt with another rebate, but it is foolhardy to cut long-term tax rates unless you are willing to cut long-term government spending by a similar amount. The deficits that result from permanent tax cuts require additional government borrowing which can drive interest rates up; higher interest rates reduce business investment spending, and if that happens, jobs can be lost.

The notion that cutting tax rates can result in increased government revenue is nonsense. If your boss tells you that he is going to increase your income by cutting your wage rate, you are probably going to see through the gimmick. Given the same number of hours worked, a lower wage rate means less earnings whereas a higher wage rate means increased earnings. Likewise, lower tax rates mean less tax revenue, and higher tax rates usually mean more revenue.

This can be seen clearly by what happened during the 1980s after the Reagan tax cut and what happened during the 1990s after the Clinton deficit-reduction package, which included higher tax rates. The Reagan tax cuts led to massive budget deficits and a quadrupling of the national debt in just 12 years. The Clinton deficit-reduction package led to a gradual elimination of budget deficits with actual budget surpluses in 1999 and 2000.

George W. Bush then pushed through another big tax cut and we had a $317.5 billion deficit in 2002 and a projected astronomical deficit of $467.6 billion for 2003. Forget about the supply-siders' theory that cuts in tax rates generate increased revenue. The theory has been tested and the results are indisputable: No amount of fuzzy math can show that lower tax rates resulted in higher revenue than would have been the case if the rates had been left unchanged.

Some die-hard Reaganites present numbers showing that tax collections were higher a few years after the Reagan tax cut than they were at the time the rates were cut. They offer the numbers as "proof" that the tax cuts resulted in higher revenue. Nice try, but they forgot something: Our economy should be growing continuously over time as the population increases and more productive resources become available. With a growing labor force and more workers paying taxes, there *should* be a substantial growth in revenue. Even when tax rates are cut, this ongoing growth in the economy will more than offset the rate cut, and revenue will increase gradually even at the lower rates.

In short, tax revenue did grow in the years after the Reagan tax cuts, but not because of them. In fact revenue did not grow nearly as fast as it would have if the tax cuts had not taken place. Revenue rose in spite of the tax cuts because of the general growth in the population and the overall economy.

By the same token, the natural growth over time in the population and the economy also results in higher government expenditures. Unless the growth in revenue keeps pace with the growth in expenditures, budget deficits will occur. It is precisely because the growth in revenue did not keep pace with the growth in expenditures after the Reagan tax cuts that the huge deficits occurred and the national debt rose from less than $1 trillion when Reagan took office to more than $4 trillion by the time George Herbert Walker Bush vacated the White House.

Likewise, it is precisely because of the deficit reduction package implemented early in the Clinton presidency that deficits were gradually reduced during his first six years and were replaced by surpluses in 1999 and 2000. And it is because of the reduction in interest rates, made possible by the deficit reductions, that during the Clinton years, the economy was able to experience the longest period of prosperity in American history.

A few decades down the road, historians will study the record of Reaganomics and the economic record under Clinton, and they will likely conclude that there must have been some kind of mass insanity in America during the transition period between the Clinton presidency and the early years of the George W. Bush presidency. How else, they will ask, can we explain that after a 20-year experiment that clearly revealed the disastrous results of supply-side economic policies under Reagan-Bush, and the positive impact of traditional economic policies under Clinton, would the nation choose to launch the new century with a return to Reaganomics?

If the historians look closely enough, they will see that the American people, who were almost totally illiterate in the area of economics, were the victims of unforgivable fraud by the administration of George W. Bush. The big lie in 2001 was that there was surplus revenue to fund the tax cut. By 2003, it should have been clear to everyone that the 2001 tax cut inflicted serious damage on both the federal budget and the economy. The talk of fantasy surpluses had given way to the reality that we were once again plunging into a deficit hole. So when Bush decided to try to push through another large tax cut in 2003, he knew the public would no longer fall for the lie that there were surplus dollars to pay for it.

THIS TIME, BUSH CHOSE to lie to the public about what effect his proposed tax cut would have on the economy and on employment, so he dubbed his proposal a "Job Creation Program," and sold it as a remedy for the high unemployment. Like all such political proposals, to make it more palatable, he included a few crumbs that would also benefit lower income families. But these portions of the cut were so small that they would do little to stimulate the economy, and the bulk of the cut would have little or no impact on job creation.

This point was made strongly by the more than 400 top economists who signed the statement in the *New York Times* on February 11, 2003. Excerpts follow from the published statement.

> . . . Regardless of how one views the specifics of the Bush plan, there is wide agreement that its purpose is a permanent change in the tax structure and not the creation of jobs and growth in the near-term . . .
>
> . . . Passing these tax cuts will worsen the long-term budget outlook, adding to the nation's projected chronic deficits. This fiscal deterioration will reduce the capacity of the government to finance Social Security and Medicare benefits as well as investments in schools, health, infrastructure, and basic research. Moreover, the proposed tax cuts will generate further inequalities in after-tax income.
>
> To be effective, a stimulus plan should rely on immediate but temporary spending and tax measures to expand demand, and it should also rely on immediate but temporary incentives for investment. Such a stimulus plan would spur growth and jobs in the short term without exacerbating the long-term budget outlook.

Economists have long been criticized by government officials for their lack of agreement on certain basic issues in government economic policy. This practice started with President Harry S. Truman, who said, "I am looking for a one-handed economist. My economists keep telling me 'On the one hand this might be the right way to go, but on the other hand . . .'" Truman wanted an economist who saw everything as black or white with no areas of gray. The problem is that there are few issues that are so clear cut that everything is black or white.

Given this reality, it is amazing that those 400 top economists, ten Nobel laureates among them, were able to agree on the wording of a statement that they could all sign. With the economists in agreement that the effect of the Bush plan would be a permanent change in the tax structure, generating further inequalities in after-tax income, and not the creation of jobs and growth in the near-term, there is a very high probability they are right.

What is the likelihood that George W. Bush would know more about any field than the top 400 experts in that field? What is the probability that George W. Bush is correct, and the 400 economists are wrong, about the potential for job creation of the Bush plan? I think that any reasonable person would have to answer that it is "almost zero."

Most Americans were probably never aware of the position and advice of the economists despite the fact that the statement appeared in the *New York Times*. It received very little national news coverage relative to the coverage President Bush got when he traveled around the country urging people to pressure their representatives in Congress to support his tax bill because it would supposedly create jobs. The president did not tell the public that most economists were opposed to the plan. He used one theme: This bill is about the creation of jobs; a vote for this bill is a vote for jobs. Given the fact that two million jobs had already been lost since Bush took office, Americans who trusted the president to tell the truth supported the bill. But even some highly respected Republican members of the Senate, who probably did not trust the president to do what was best for America, opposed the measure. Nevertheless, after much arm-twisting and deception, Bush managed to squeak his tax cut through Congress with the tie-breaking vote of Vice President Cheney.

Enactment of both the 2001 and the 2003 Bush tax cuts were accomplished only by engaging in fraud against the American people. Fraud is very broadly defined for purposes of both civil and criminal litigation. An excerpt from the article on fraud in *Encyclopedia Americana* follows.

> Generally fraud involves the intentional misrepresentation of a material fact, resulting in damage to the victim. So defined, fraud may form the basis of a civil action for damages or of a criminal prosecution . . . Although fraud is often perpetrated by means of actual statements that misrepresent facts, deception that constitutes fraud can be practiced by concealment, by half-truths calculated to deceive, or tricks or devices that mislead the victim. Also, a statement made recklessly without knowing its truth or falsity may, if false, constitute a fraud.

Certainly Bush's actions to push both tax bills through Congress fall under the criteria of fraud as defined in the preceding excerpt. The president pushed the 2001 tax cut on the basis of alleged large surpluses as far as the eye could see. There were no such surpluses, and the president had to have known this by the time his proposal came up for a vote. He was clearly guilty of "intentional misrepresentation of a material fact resulting in damage to the victim," the victim in this case being the millions of Americans who will be adversely affected by the tax cut's repercussions.

In summary, the Bush tax cuts of 2001 and 2003 will cause massive additional future deficits and push the size of the national debt to astronomical new levels. They create additional inequalities in after-tax incomes, and they do little to create jobs. Bush could have used one-time tax rebates to restore the economy to full employment at only a tiny fraction of the cost of the tax cuts that were passed, and such one-time rebates would have had little negative effect on the long-term budget outlook.

Bush chose to push the tax cuts through, not in an effort to help the economy, but because they were an integral part of his hidden agenda to greatly reduce the size and scope of the federal government. (The tax cuts also provided a way for Bush to reward his richest campaign contributors.) Reagan had tried to starve the government into becoming much leaner by cutting off part of the revenue flow with his big tax cuts. However, Reagan's plan backfired. Instead of decreasing spending by the amount of the tax cuts, Congress chose to replace the lost tax revenue by borrowing, and increasing the size of the national debt. Instead of the "tax and spend" policies that Democrats were so often accused of, the Republicans chose to launch a new era that would follow the policy of "borrow and spend."

CHAPTER EIGHT

The Hidden Agenda

~

*Government is not reason, it is not eloquence—it is force! Like fire it
is a dangerous servant and a fearful master; never for a moment
should it be left to irresponsible action.*

—George Washington

$\mathcal{R}$ONALD REAGAN BROUGHT ABOUT many changes in
America and left a legacy of huge budget deficits and a soaring national debt, but Reagan failed to achieve the goal that was
probably most dear to his heart—the dismantling of the federal government as we know it. Reagan hated big government and was determined to bring about a major downsizing. He had a plan that he
thought would accomplish that goal; it was to cut taxes by so much
that when the deficits began to soar, Congress would be forced to dismantle major government programs. Without funds to sustain them,
the social programs he despised so much would starve to death.

Reagan seemed to think he could cut government spending by simply reducing taxes and thus cutting back on the government's
"allowance," but he underestimated the determination of members of
Congress to spend on programs they believed in, whether the revenue
was there or not. In addition, Reagan himself was unwilling to cut
back on defense spending, so the reduction in tax revenue that resulted
from the big tax cuts was not offset by similar reductions in spending.
The national debt quadrupled during the Reagan-Bush years, but

spending continued, and the deficit during the last year of George Herbert Walker Bush's presidency was at an all time record high of $340.5 billion.

With the election of Bill Clinton in 1992, the attempt to downsize the federal government ended. The Clinton deficit-reduction package eliminated the huge deficits, and Clinton actively tried to make government a more responsive servant of the American people. At the beginning of his first term, he even pursued a controversial campaign to establish a national health care system, but he failed to get it enacted into law.

Al Gore strongly believed that the government should play an active role in improving the lives of American citizens, and if he had been elected in 2000, we would have seen increased spending on both education and health care programs during his administration. With the election so close that the outcome was ultimately decided by the United States Supreme Court, and given the fact that Gore received around 500,000 more popular votes than Bush, it would be hard for anyone to make a strong rational argument that President George W. Bush had a mandate from the people to bring about major changes in America.

Although the scandal in Clinton's personal life cost him a lot of support, the American people continued to strongly support his domestic and economic policies. Because the country prospered during his presidency, many political analysts believe that if Clinton had been eligible to run for another term, he would have been reelected.

By no stretch of the imagination could the 2000 election of President Bush have been considered a mandate for any major change in United States policy; thus, it was impossible for him to launch a direct, open campaign to downsize the government. He would not have been able to get the support for such action from either the Congress or the American people. But getting public support for major tax cuts was a different story, and Bush saw this as an alternative route to dismantling big government.

Like Reagan, George W. Bush is no fan of the federal government.

Like most conservative governors, when he was governor of Texas, he came to despise the restraints placed on state government by the federal government, and his decision to seek the presidency must have been at least partly motivated by his desire to trim the federal government's size.

In order to get elected Bush needed the support of the ultraconservative wing of the Republican party as well as the Christian Coalition and other Christian right organizations. He actively cultivated the support of the Christian right and ultimately became their de facto leader. In an article entitled, "Religious Right Finds Its Center in Oval Office," that appeared in the December 24, 2001, issue of the *Washington Post,* writer Dana Milbank describes Bush's rise to leadership of the conservative Christian organization. Milbank writes, "Pat Robertson's resignation this month as president of the Christian Coalition confirmed the ascendance of a new leader of the religious right in America: George W. Bush."

Milbank quoted Gary Bauer, a religious conservative who challenged Bush in the Republican primary, as saying, "I think Robertson stepped down because the position has already been filled . . . There was already a great deal of identification with the president before 9-11 in the world of the Christian right, and the nature of this war is such that it's heightened the sense that a man of God is in the White House."

Ralph Reed, who once led the Christian Coalition and now is chairman of the Georgia Republican Party, contends, according to Milbank, that conservative Christians tend to view Bush's success as part of a divine plan. In the article, Dana Milbank quotes Ralph Reed as saying, "I've heard a lot of 'God knew something we didn't.' In the evangelical mind, the notion of an omniscient God is central to their theology. He had a knowledge nobody else had: He knew George Bush had the ability to lead in this compelling way."

Given this historically unique relationship between the President of the United States and the Christian right, which Bush needs to be reelected in 2004, the agenda of the Christian Coalition pretty much becomes the agenda of President George W. Bush. In choosing Dick Cheney as his running mate, and endorsing a Republican national platform that catered to the extreme right wing of the party at the time of the Republican National Convention, Bush satisfied Christian conservatives who had demanded a staunchly social conservative vice president and platform in return for their support. The Christian Coalition announced at the convention that they would distribute 75 million voter guides and mobilize churches to make George W. Bush the next president of the United States.

Bush uses the term "compassionate conservatism" to describe his right-wing agenda. These two words contradict each other. There is nothing compassionate about true conservative ideology. Over the years, conservatives have consistently opposed programs to help the poor and the disadvantaged. They have opposed programs designed to provide greater equality of opportunity. They have favored cutting benefits to the disadvantaged in order to provide tax cuts to the rich, and they have been more concerned about the profits of large corporations than about the incomes of ordinary Americans.

Compassionate conservatism is just another Trojan horse, another deceitful way to bring about change that the people would not support on its own merits. Bush is determined to impose his own views and those of right-wing conservatives on the American people—no matter how much fraud is required to accomplish the task. In a speech in San Jose, California, on April 30, 2002, Bush revealed his desire for limited government. Excerpts from the speech follow.

> We are a generous and caring people. We don't believe in a sink-or-swim society. The policies of our government must heed the universal call of all faiths to love a neighbor as we would want to be loved ourselves. We need a different approach than either big government or indifferent government. We need a government that is focused, effective, and close to the people; a government that does a few things, and does them well.

There is no mistaking Bush's view of the role of government. When he says, "We need a government . . . that does a few things and does them well," he is signaling his intention to trim the size and scope of government. Bush goes on to explain his philosophy of "compassionate conservatism":

> Government cannot solve every problem, but it can encourage people and communities to help themselves and to help one another. Often the truest kind of compassion is to help citizens build lives of their own. I call my philosophy and approach "compassionate conservatism." It is compassionate to actively help our fellow citizens in need. It is conservative to insist on responsibility and on results. And with this hopeful approach we can make a real difference in people's lives.

Bush's approach is nothing more than to have the government turn its back on the most disadvantaged Americans and call it compassionate. His approach is to take the money targeted for programs for the poor, give it to the wealthy in the form of tax cuts, and call it conservative.

So what is the real reason for the huge Bush tax cuts? It is certainly not to help the economy or the budget; they will harm both the economy and the budget. It is certainly not because the government has surplus money; the government has never been so much in the red. I believe the tax cuts are a deliberate effort to put the finances of the United States government in such dire straights that Congress will be forced to dismantle the social safety net. I believe the purpose of the tax cuts is to intentionally create a financial crisis unlike anything the United States has ever before faced. Under such conditions, it may be possible for the conservatives to accomplish things they could never accomplish through the democratic process.

The Reagan tax cuts created a situation in which the tax system was not capable, under any circumstances, of generating enough revenue to balance the budget. The Clinton deficit reduction package partially fixed the problem, and in 1999 and 2000 the nation was able to experience non-Social Security surpluses for the first time in 40 years. However, in 2001, as the economy slipped into recession, the deficits returned.

In short, before George W. Bush took office and began pursuing tax cuts, the tax rates were already insufficient to generate a balanced budget except under the extraordinary circumstances of 1999 and 2000; the peak of the business cycle and the lowest unemployment rate in 30 years. In 2001, there was no wiggle room for even small tax cuts. If Bush had left tax rates as they were, the government would probably still have run deficits in most years, but the deficits would have been small enough that they would not have posed a major threat to the budget or to economic stability. However, even a small *reduction* in tax rates would have almost guaranteed budget deficits in each and every year.

At the time Bush took over the reins of government, the economy was in the best shape ever, with unemployment at historic lows. There was still the fact that the national debt had increased from $1 trillion in 1981 to more than $6 trillion by 2001, but because of the budget surpluses in 1999 and 2000, the national debt was not growing at the time Clinton left office.

Bush inherited the best economy in American history, and the old expression, "If it ain't broke, don't fix it," applied to the American economy more than ever before as we entered the new century. Yet Bush seemed determined to break the economy so that it would *need* to be fixed. Despite widespread opposition, he pushed his 2001 $1.35 trillion tax cut through, promising that it would not mean a return to deficits or the pirating of any of the Social Security surplus.

By 2003, it was clear that both the economy and the budget outlook had deteriorated, rather than improved, as Bush had predicted. The 2002 non-Social Security deficit was a whopping $317.5 billion, and the projected deficit for 2003 was $467.6 billion. Instead of admitting he had been wrong, and calling for repeal of the 2001 tax cut, Bush's prescription was for more of the same medicine that had already done so much damage to both the economy and the federal budget.

This time Bush claimed the tax cut would stimulate the economy and create jobs. He knew it would create few new jobs, and that it would lead to even higher deficits, but what did that matter? It would just speed up the impending crisis which would enable him to dismantle the government social programs he so loathed. Such a day of reckoning is an absolute certainty.

- As the deficits become larger and larger, and the government has to borrow more and more money, interest rates are bound to be forced up.
- Higher interest rates will serve as a drag on the economy and lead to higher unemployment.
- As the unemployment rises and fewer Americans have jobs, government tax revenue will decline even more, and automatic government spending programs such as unemployment compensation will rise.
- The decline in tax revenue and increase in government spending will result in even larger deficits.

Of course, Bush paints a very different picture of the future, but the evidence continues to build that, a little farther down the road, budget deficits will be so large as to be overwhelming. An article in the May 29, 2003, *New York Times* reveals the shocking results of a study commissioned by the United States Treasury that shows the United States currently faces a future of chronic federal budget deficits totaling at least $44,200 billion. According to the article:

> The study's analysis of future deficits dwarfs previous estimates of the financial challenge facing Washington. It is roughly equivalent to 10 times the publicly held national debt, four years of U.S. economic output or more than 94 percent of all U.S. household assets.

The study was commissioned by then-Treasury Secretary Paul

O'Neill, who was fired by Bush in December 2002. It was conducted by Kent Smetters, then-Treasury deputy assistant secretary for economic policy; and Jagdessh Gokhale, then a consultant to the Treasury. Gokhale, now an economist for the Cleveland Federal Reserve Bank said: "When we were conducting the study, my impression was that it was slated to appear (in the Budget). At some point, the momentum builds and you think everything is a go, and then the decision came down that we weren't part of the prospective budget."

The Bush administration chose to exclude the study findings from the annual budget report for fiscal year 2004, which was published in February 2003. At the time, the president was actively campaigning for his 2003 tax cut, keeping the public in the dark as much as possible as to the outlook for future deficits. It is easy to understand why Bush would not want the public to know about this report. *[It estimates that closing the gap between revenue and expenditures would require the equivalent of an immediate and permanent 66 percent across-the-board income tax increase.]*

The dire predictions of this study, along with all the warnings from top economists against enacting the 2003 tax cut, should have been more than enough to make Bush reconsider the tax cut, or at least put it on the back burner, if he were truly concerned about the future of America and its citizens. Instead, he used pressure tactics and anything else at his disposal to get the cut through Congress. Upon signing the bill into law on Wednesday June 4, 2003, Bush said:

> We can say loud and clear to the American people: You got more of your own money to spend so that this economy can get a good wind behind it.

It is hard to find any rationalization to account for the unaffordable Bush tax cuts except that they will starve the federal budget and require major spending cuts. As defense spending is not a likely candidate for cutbacks, and interest on the national debt must be paid in order for the government to be able to continue to borrow, spending cuts would most likely fall on Social Security, Medicare, other health programs, and public education.

Since the large Social Security surpluses, earmarked for the coming retirement surge, have already been borrowed by the government and spent on other programs, there will be a terrible crunch in both the Social Security and Medicare programs. Unless the government raises taxes in order to repay the massive amounts of money it has borrowed from the Social Security trust fund, there would have to be major cutbacks in both Social Security and Medicare benefits. One of the most likely scenarios is that these programs would become welfare programs for the most needy Americans, while benefits for the less needy may be completely cut or at least greatly reduced.

The democratic principles of the United States dictate that the public make the decisions as to what role government should play in their lives, and what government programs should exist. Conservatives have fought Social Security and Medicare since they were founded, but so far, they have not been able to harm or eliminate these programs because there is wide public support for them. Having been unable to dismantle the programs through the open, democratic system, conservatives have turned to underhanded, back-door methods of attacking them.

Beginning with the Reagan administration, conservatives have tried to cut back on government funding for Social Security and Medicare by reducing revenue to the point where spending would *have* to be cut. Reagan promised that his tax-cut program would lead to a balanced budget by 1984 and pledged not to make any major cuts in government services; the promise was doomed to be broken. It is not possible to have major tax cuts without matching those cuts, dollar for dollar, with program cuts. Reagan thought the program cuts would come later, when revenue became insufficient to fund them, but few programs *were* cut. The net result was a quadrupling of the national debt in just 12 years.

The deficits were brought under control during the Clinton administration, but George W. Bush almost immediately threw the budget back into deficit territory with his $1.35 trillion 2001 tax cut. He then added insult to injury by pushing through the additional $350 billion cut of 2003. Conditions are very different today than they were at the time of the Reagan tax cuts. The public is more conscious, and more critical, of massive deficit spending. They showed only limited support for the Bush tax cuts, and they will demand that some kind of action be taken when it becomes obvious that the deficits are out of control. The only options will be major cuts in programs, large tax increases, or some combination of the two.

This attempt to eliminate social programs by cutting off their funding source by devious means is the granddaddy of all frauds. It violates everything that American democracy stands for. It is the people—not the president—who hold the power to decide what programs they want and how much in taxes they are willing to pay for these programs. It is the people, through their elected representatives, who decide the appropriate role of government. And it is the people who have the authority to choose whether to turn back the clock to an era rejected by the majority of Americans long ago, or move forward to an era in which the American dream is possible for more and more of the people.

Every American citizen, and every business, knows that there is no free lunch. They know that if we want to spend more, we must earn more. And they know that if we cut back on our income we will have to make sacrifices and reduce our spending. Those who fail to recognize the basic principle that it is not possible to spend more than one's income over the long run hear the message loud and clear when they end up in bankruptcy court.

Every wage-earner knows that a cut in wages ultimately means a reduction in his or her standard of living. And every American family knows that there are two ways to throw a balanced budget into deficit: One way is to increase spending without increasing income; the other way is to decrease income without simultaneously reducing spending.

Perhaps it is a slight exaggeration to say that all Americans and all

Karl Rove is President George W. Bush's top political adviser. He has been close to the Bush family for decades, having first worked for former President Bush in 1973. He has been George W. Bush's top adviser since Bush announced his intention to run for governor of Texas in November 1993. Rove is considered by both Democrats and Republicans to be one of the most brilliant and successful political consultants of all time.

Many critics believe that Rove has too much power and influence over Bush. According to most analysts, Bush never makes a decision without first consulting with Karl Rove, and it is believed that many of Bush's ideas and policies originated with Rove. More and more critics are charging that Rove—not George W. Bush—is actually the most powerful man in America because of the enormous influence Rove has on Bush.

Two veteran Texas newsmen, James Moore and Wayne Slater, who have covered the phenomenal rise to power of Karl Rove for more than 15 years, have published a new book entitled, *Bush's Brain: How Karl Rove Made George W. Bush Presidential.* This is quite a tribute to the power and influence of Karl Rove, who is not just one of Bush's advisers, but his top adviser.

Rove has been immersed in Republican politics ever since he made a decision to back Nixon when he was nine years old. He left the University of Utah in 1971, without graduating, to become executive director of the College Republicans. He is alleged to have been a part of the "dirty-tricks" team in Nixon's 1972 campaign. According to Rove's classmates at Olympus High School in Salt Lake City, it was clear even then that Rove was headed for Washington. Moore and Slater report that Karl's sister Reba said, "Karl was consumed by politics at an early age," and that "He was always going to be president."

Rove has a reputation for winning at all costs, and on his journey to reach the pinnacle of power, there were many casualties among his opponents. His decisions seem to be motivated more by political considerations, in terms of how voters will react to an issue than by anything else. It is not clear whether Rove has veto power over the proposals coming from other presidential advisers, but the other advisers clearly do not possess power equal to Rove's.

Most past occupants of the White House have had an inner circle of political advisers with roughly equal power and access to the president. No single adviser has ever been indispensable, and those who became overly ambitious or assertive did not stay in the inner circle very long.

Given Rove's apparently unique status in the Bush administration, it is not clear whether it would be feasible for Bush to fire him if circumstances arose that justified such action. Many believe that without Karl Rove there would never have been a President George W. Bush, and they doubt that Bush could perform his duties effectively without his right-hand man beside him. If this is true, it raises serious Constitutional questions about the powers of the elected president.

families know these fundamental principles of finance; some appear to be ignorant of them. One such person is George W. Bush. He does not seem to understand these basic principles. His explanations for why he wants to cut taxes range from, "the government has more money than it needs," to the notion that taxes are too high, or too unfair. He talks about taxes as if he were talking about a moral issue: Taxes are bad, and tax cuts are good. Nobody should have to pay so much in taxes, and it's unfair to tax income twice. Having been born into wealth, and never having had to worry about making ends meet, it is possible that Bush really doesn't see the connection between the need to cut expenditures when taxes are cut. But one would think that somewhere in his MBA curriculum he would have learned about the need to balance budgets, at least in the long run.

Actually, I think Bush is just playing dumb. If he didn't learn it on his own, certainly Karl Rove (the man described as Bush's brain) has explained how finances work. There is no question that Bush knows his tax cuts will result in the need for major spending cuts. His failure to acknowledge this fact, and to list his top candidates for the chopping block, is fraud in and of itself. George W. Bush's vision of the future may be quite different from that of the majority of the American people, and he has no right to try to force his vision on the rest of America.

CHAPTER NINE

Wealth, Privilege, and Power

❧

Two maggots riding on a workman's shovel accidentally fell off. By pure chance, one fell into a rich pile of garbage while the other one fell into a crack in the sidewalk. The fortunate maggot became fat and sleek in his rich environment. One day he crawled away from his rich garbage pile to the crack in the sidewalk. As he peered down into the crack, he found himself staring into the emaciated face of his former fellow traveler, who had subsisted on a few crumbs that occasionally fell into the crack. The thin, starving maggot asked in a weak voice from the lower depths, "How is it, my friend, that you're so prosperous and fat, while I am near starvation?" The disdainful reply came booming back: "Ha! Brains and hard work!"

—A story out of the Great Depression of the 1930s.

*G*EORGE W. BUSH'S RISE to the presidency is the antithesis of the American Dream. It is not the result of exceptional talent, hard work, and perseverance. It is more akin to an ascension to the throne when one is born into the ruling family of a country.

Bush is President of the United States today only because of the power that wealth and privilege bestow upon any person born into affluence in this modern era of mass communications. Had George W. Bush been born in the era of Abraham Lincoln, no amount of money could have put him in the White House. About the only advantage that money could buy for a candidate during Lincoln's time was a faster horse that would get the candidate from one town to another in less time so he could give more stump speeches per day than his opponent. There was no way to reach a mass audience then, no matter how large a campaign chest one had.

There is little evidence that George W. Bush set his sights on the White House at an early age and diligently worked toward that goal, as is true of some former presidents. When he entered Harvard Business School at age 27, he confided to a friend that he had no idea what he wanted to do with the rest of his life. George W. Bush had run for Congress in 1978, but lost; that experience apparently soured Bush on politics, because he didn't seek public office again until 16 years later when he ran for governor of Texas in 1994. One would have expected a man with a burning desire for a career in public service to have pulled himself up after the 1978 defeat and plunged right back into the political fray. But he didn't. Instead, he tried to strike it rich in the oil drilling business.

In 1986, shortly before his 40th birthday, Bush sold his failing oil company and did some real soul searching as to what he should do with his life. Although he had worked on his father's political campaigns, he had not sought any other political office for himself since 1978. But, he was now thinking about a possible political career. He would consider running for governor of Texas.

When George H. W. Bush was defeated by Bill Clinton in 1992, George W.'s political ambitions took on a new dimension. He would avenge his father's defeat and become president himself. This was a pretty ambitious goal for someone who had never held any public office, who had been rejected by the University of Texas Law School, and who had failed in business. But then George W. Bush wasn't just anyone. He was the son of a United States president and a member of a powerful political family. In addition, he had access to almost unlimited money for waging an aggressive and expensive campaign to unseat popular incumbent Texas Governor Ann Richards.

Despite the uphill battle, Bush and Karl Rove managed to unseat Richards. Four years later, in 1998, Bush was easily reelected to a second term as governor of Texas. He now had a launching pad for his bid for the presidency.

The rest is history. Bush was able to raise so much money for his campaign for the presidency that other candidates for the Republican nomination stood little chance against him. In essence, Bush bought the Republican nomination. And when the fall election ended up being decided by the United States Supreme Court, two of the justices who made the historic decision had been appointed to the court by Bush's father. Three others had been appointed by Ronald Reagan. In short, Bush's road to the presidency was paved with wealth, privilege, and power.

I doubt that Bush could mentally put himself in the shoes of a person who was born into poverty, attended mediocre public schools, and had no connections whatsoever with anyone in a higher socioeconomic position who could put in a good word to a potential employer. And Bush could not know what it is like to be hungry or unable to properly clothe his children. Waiting in long job lines in an effort to land a job would be totally foreign to President Bush.

President Bush has lived a very privileged life and doesn't seem to be able to identify with the vast majority of Americans who have not lived such lives. Instead of pushing an agenda that would make life easier for middle- and lower-income individuals, Bush seems determined to further help the privileged at the expense of the disadvantaged.

Wealthy families that become actively involved in American politics usually take one of two pathways. Either they try to bring about more equality and champion the causes of the disadvantaged, or they try to widen the gap between the rich and the poor, making their lives and the lives of other members of their class even better at the expense of the nonprivileged.

The Roosevelt and the Kennedy families seemed to be very conscious of their privileged status, and they worked hard to make life better for all Americans. The Bush family members seem to see others in their socioeconomic class as their primary constituents, and seem to have little social conscience. The gap between the rich and the poor is so wide in the United States that there can be no justification for government policies that further widen the gap. Many people believe the gap should be reduced, but at the very least, it is time to put the brakes on programs that take from the poor and give to the rich. This Robin Hood-in-reverse policy is not consistent with the American dream.

Table 6 shows the portion of the nation's total income going to each fifth of the population in 1970 and 2001, and the gain or loss by each group during the 31-year period. In 1970, the lowest income fifth (20 percent) of the population received 4.1 percent of the nation's total income. The highest fifth (20 percent) of the population received 43.3 percent of the nation's income in 1970. Keep in mind that these two groups are equal in size. They each constitute 20 percent of the nation's population, and if income distribution were totally equal, they would each get 20 percent of the nation's income. In 1970, the highest income fifth of the population received more than ten times as much income as the lowest income fifth received.

No reasonable person would argue for totally equal distribution of income. Some people contribute a great deal more resources to the economy than others, so it is only fair that they receive a larger share of

TABLE 6: INCOME OF AMERICAN FAMILIES AND PERCENTAGE LOSS OR GAIN, 1970-2001			
Income Rank	1970	2001	Percent Loss(-) or Gain(+) 1970-2001
Lowest Fifth	4.1	3.5	-.6
Second Fifth	10.8	8.7	-2.1
Third Fifth	17.4	14.6	-2.8
Fourth Fifth	24.5	23.0	-1.5
Highest Fifth	43.3	50.1	+6.8

Source: U.S. Bureau of the Census, Current Population Reports

the nation's income than those who contribute substantially less. In addition to the issue of fairness, there is the issue of economic incentives. There must always be some gap between the rich and the poor so the poor will have economic incentives to work harder in an effort to move up the income ladder. The crucial question is how wide the gap must be to provide sufficient economic incentives. Personally, I believe the gap was more than sufficient in 1970, when the highest-income 20 percent of the population was receiving more than 10 times as much as the lowest-income 20 percent. In fact, if there was any argument for changing the size of the gap, I would have argued for narrowing it.

Now look at how income distribution changed between 1970 and 2001. In 2001, the lowest-income fifth of the population received only 3.5 percent of the nation's income, whereas the highest-income fifth received 50.1 percent. In 2001 the highest-income fifth of the population received more than 14 times as much income as the lowest-income fifth, as compared with only about 10 times as much in 1970. Clearly, the rich got richer and the poor got poorer during the 31-year period, 1970-2001.

A closer look at the numbers reveals something that may be startling to many Americans in the middle income group. Not only did the poorest fifth become poorer, but the second fifth, the third fifth, and the fourth fifth also received a smaller percentage of the nation's income in 2001 than they had in 1970. If the bottom 80 percent were losers, who were the winners? The highest income fifth of the nation's population received 50.1 percent of the nation's income in 2001 as compared to only 43.3 percent in 1970.

The Robin Hood-in-reverse policies of recent decades have not only taken from the poor and given to the rich, they have also taken from the bottom 80 percent of American families and given the money to the most affluent 20 percent of the population. These trends are almost totally due to the policies of Reagan and George H.W. Bush, because the assault on the lower- and middle-income Americans by George W. Bush would not have had time to show up in the 2001 numbers. The higher tax rates for the super rich under Clinton probably moderated the trend a bit, but their effects were diminished by the huge tax breaks the rich had had under Reagan.

When we look at after-tax income distribution, we find that the Reagan tax cuts, which created such huge deficits and sent the national debt soaring, have benefited the wealthy at the expense of the lower- and middle-income groups even more than the preceding Census Bureau data suggests. A report, "The Widening Income Gulf," released by the Center on Budget and Policy Priorities on September 9, 1999, demonstrates just how distorted after-tax income had become long before George W. Bush had the opportunity to distort it even more. The following are excerpts from the report.

> Congressional Budget Office data issued this summer indicate that after-tax income has increased dramatically since 1977 for the highest-income one percent of the population but risen only modestly for those in the middle of the income spectrum and declined for those in the bottom fifth. The CBO data which start in 1977 and include projections for 1999, are widely regarded by analysts as the best data available on income and tax trends . . .
>
> . . . among the top 20 percent of households, average after-tax income is projected to increase a robust 43 percent in the 1977-1999 period. Among the top one percent of households, average after-tax income is projected to more than double, jumping 115 percent . . .
>
> . . . Income disparities have widened to such a degree that in 1999, the richest one percent of the population is projected to receive as much after-tax income as the bottom 38 percent combined. That is, the 2.7 million Americans with the largest incomes are expected to receive as much after-tax income as the 100 million Americans with the lowest incomes.

This is a startling revelation. The 2.7 million Americans with the highest incomes would receive as much after-tax income as the 100 million lowest-income Americans. The report goes on to point out that much of the increase in the after-tax income of the top one percent of the population is the result of net tax cuts that high-income households have received since the late 1970s.

During the Clinton administration, even with the tax increases on high-income households, the tax burdens on the richest one percent of households were substantially lower than they had been in 1977. The report points out just how much better off the wealthy were in 1999 than they were in 1977 in terms of taxes paid.

> . . . If the richest one percent of households paid the same percentage of income in federal taxes in 1999 as this group paid in 1977, these households would pay an average of at least $40,000 more in taxes this year. In other words, these households have received an average tax cut of more than $40,000. This $40,000-plus average tax cut for the top one percent of households is greater than the entire average before-tax income of the middle fifth of households, which is projected to be $38,700 per household in 1999.

George W. Bush must be extremely proud of what he has pulled off on behalf of his family and all the other wealthy families in America. The richest Americans were already paying $40,000 per year less in taxes in 1999 than they were paying in 1977, and George W. has given them major additional tax relief at the expense of the future of this nation. I wonder just how many of those 2.7 million richest Americans gave part or all of their $40,000 tax relief to the George W. Bush presidential campaign. Those who did got a tremendous return on their investment in the form of new tax savings, and we can be absolutely sure that a substantial portion of the new tax relief money will be invested in the reelection campaign for George W. Bush.

In a sense, today, the United States presidency is for sale to the highest bidder. Ross Perot tried to buy his way into the White House, and he might have succeeded if he had spent all of his money. But Perot wasn't willing to sacrifice all his loot for the job. George W. Bush doesn't have to spend much, if any, of his personal money, because he has many wealthy "friends" who know a good investment when they see it.

The intent of our founding fathers was that each American would have equal voting power, and therefore public policy would reflect the will of the majority. They could not have envisioned how the advent of radio and television would give wealthy candidates an enormous advantage over those who lacked wealth, because the wealthy can buy access to voters in the form of TV campaign commercials. Thus, instead of the principle of one-person-one-vote, the American political system operates more on a one-dollar-one-vote principle. By no stretch of the imagination can such a system be considered democratic. We are a lot closer to plutocracy (which is defined as "government by the wealthy") than we are to true democracy.

Webster's New World Dictionary gives five definitions for democracy. They are: (1) government in which the people hold the ruling power either directly or through elected representatives; (2) a country, state, etc. with such government; (3) majority rule; (4) the principle of equality of rights, opportunity, and treatment, or the practice of this principle; (5) the common people, especially as the wielders of political power.

Does America currently fit *any* of these definitions of democracy? I don't think so. Definition (4) comes the closest to what I have always thought American democracy was supposed to be. We have equality of rights guaranteed by the Constitution, but these rights are often violated. How about equality of opportunity and treatment? Did every Texan have an equal opportunity to become governor, or was this opportunity available only to those who either had personal wealth or wealthy backers? Did every would-be candidate for the Republican presidential nomination have an equal opportunity to get the nomination, or did George W. Bush have the nomination sewed up from the very beginning because of his family connections and the massive amounts of money that came his way?

Now look at the definition of another, less familiar, political term in *Webster's New World Dictionary*: plutocracy. There are only two definitions for this term. (1) government by the wealthy; and (2) a group of wealthy people who control or influence a government. Isn't the definition of plutocracy a far more accurate definition of the American government in the twenty-first century than any of the definitions of democracy?

Most Americans have never heard the term "plutocracy." Yet, most Americans would agree that the wealthy have undue influence in the American political system, and they know that wealthy people do try to influence or control government. President Bush talks of bringing democracy to Iraq and other countries. Is he really trying to impose a form of government on other countries that he does not support for the United States? Or is it plutocracy that he really wants to impose on foreign nations? It is a lot easier to control a foreign government made up of a few wealthy people than it is to control the majority of the people where majority rule is in effect.

The future of this great and treasured nation that we love so much is in great jeopardy today because, to a large extent, the government has come under the control of the wealthy. The Bush tax cuts are not good for America or for the majority of Americans. But they are very good for those 2.7 million Americans who make up the highest-income one percent of the population. The evidence is clear that over the past two decades the lowest-income 80 percent of the population has been losing ground to the highest-income 20 percent, and mostly to the top one percent. If we had true democracy and an informed electorate, how could those richest 20 percent impose their will over the other 80 percent?

In summary, the concentration of wealth, privilege, and power in the hands of the elite is the greatest threat of all to the future of American democracy. In an effort to please the wealthy, and hold on to their financial support, our government has passed special legislation that is favorable to the wealthy but harmful to the public in general and to the future of America. We must have major campaign reform that will prevent the wealthy from buying public office or political favors from elected officials. We must rescue America from plutocracy and return it to the treasured democracy that our founding fathers envisioned.

CHAPTER TEN

The Impending Crises

~

In just two years, America has thus witnessed a $10 trillion projected deficit swing—undoubtedly the biggest swing in fiscal expectation in U.S. history other than during years of total war. There are times, to be sure, when deficits today can be justified by surpluses tomorrow. But right now the long-term deficit outlook is even worse than the 10-year outlook. Let's keep in mind that we face an unfunded obligation for Social Security, Medicare and federal pensions of $25 trillion . . . A future of mounting deficits is a cause for grave concern. Mounting deficits can slow and even halt the steady growth in material living standards that has always nourished the American Dream. When such deficits are incurred in order to fund a rising transfer from young to old, they also constitute an injustice against future generations.

—Peter G. Peterson, President of the Concord Coalition and former U.S. Secretary of Commerce, [Testimony before U.S. House Committee on Financial Services, April 30, 2003]

*W*HEN RONALD REAGAN TOOK over the reins of government in 1981, the total accumulation of debt by the previous 39 administrations over 192 years of our history had not yet reached $1 trillion. The grand total was $932 billion.

Although a trillion dollars is not an insignificant amount, the fact that it had taken 192 years to approach the first $1 trillion of debt was somewhat comforting, so the national debt was not seen as one of the major problems facing America when Reagan became president. That all changed very quickly. In just a little over five years, Reagan doubled the national debt. And by the time George Herbert Walker Bush vacated the White House, the national debt had soared to more than $4 trillion. In just 12 years, the Reagan-Bush administrations quadrupled the $1 trillion national debt that had accumulated over 192 years!

In 1992, President Bush was defeated by Bill Clinton, primarily because of the massive deficits, the soaring national debt, and the weak economy. Through higher taxes and reduced government spending, Clinton reversed the trend. The deficits got smaller and smaller during Clinton's first six years, and the government experienced non-Social Security surpluses in 1999 and 2000 for the first time in 40 years.

However, the elimination of deficits by Clinton did nothing to undo the gigantic national debt that, by the time Clinton left office, had risen above the $6 trillion mark. We were spending approximately $1 billion per day just to pay the interest on the huge debt, which at that time was more than we were spending on national defense. Also, as Clinton left office, the government owed more than a trillion dollars to the Social Security trust fund. Like his predecessor, Clinton had spent Social Security surplus funds that were supposed to be saved for the retirement of the baby boomers on general operating expenses.

When Clinton left office, the nation was far from trouble-free but, if a return to deficits could be avoided, and if the debt to the Social Security trust fund could gradually be repaid, it looked like the nation just might find its way to long-term solvency. But the entire financial picture was fragile, and it would take extremely sound and responsible economic and budget policies over the course of the next two decades to avoid a financial calamity.

Putting George W. Bush in charge of such a difficult and delicate task was like turning a bull loose in a china shop. He came storming into office pushing for policies that were almost the exact opposite of what the economy needed. And he seemed determined to undo all the accomplishments of the Clinton years.

America will pay dearly for these antics of George W. Bush, and historians will probably describe him as a president who placed a higher priority on attaining political objectives than he did on looking out for the welfare of America and its citizens. But historians will also be critical of the United States Congress and the American public in general for allowing Bush to take action that was so clearly detrimental to America's future. This is not a case of evenly divided opinion. Almost all the economic experts warned against this action; under these circumstances, Bush bears most of the responsibility for the consequences we will all suffer as a result of his economic actions.

There is not just a single economic crisis down the road for America. There are multiple crises that will hit at different points along the road. I see at least three crises that are directly related to government fraud and irresponsible economic policies. They are:

(1) the consumer confidence crisis
(2) the crisis of artificially high interest rates
(3) the crisis of Social Security insolvency

The consumer-confidence crisis was discussed briefly in Chapter 6. I pointed out in that chapter that it started shortly after George W. Bush became president because of Bush's knack for issuing public statements that made consumers jittery. At times when consumers are confident that their jobs are secure and the national economy is sound, they spend a good portion of whatever income they have on a regular basis. However, during periods of uncertainty, when consumers fear loss of their jobs, they reduce their spending and begin saving for the possible forthcoming crisis.

When consumers curtail their spending, retailers send fewer new orders to producers. As orders decline, companies cut back on production and lay off workers. As laid-off workers reduce their spending, still more workers will lose their jobs. Therefore, one of the most important responsibilities of any president is to instill confidence in consumers so they will continue buying the output of workers.

President Bush has done a terrible job of inspiring consumer confidence. Granted, we have faced one of the greatest national security crises in our history in the form of the September 11, 2001, terrorist attacks, and that has played a major role in consumer confidence. However, consumer confidence was extremely low before the terrorist attack. The Bush administration would like the public to blame all economic problems on September 11, and therefore avoid any responsibility for them, but the record shows otherwise.

If the terrorist attacks and the war against Iraq had never taken place, our economy would still be in deep trouble today because of the Bush administration's economic policies. Economic problems were approaching the crisis level and dominating the news before September 11, and would have been the country's major running news story for the last two years. The war against terrorism and the war against Iraq shifted the focus of Americans away from the economy, and the news media did hardly any economic reporting during the Iraq war.

To illustrate just how preoccupied America was with the problems of our economy prior to September 11, I have reproduced excerpts from the *New York Times* and the *Washington Post* from the month prior to the horrendous events of September 11.

BUSH PROJECTIONS SHOW SHARP DROP IN BUDGET SURPLUS

By Richard W. Stevenson (NYT August 23, 2001)
Ending a brief but giddy era of fiscal plenty, the Bush administration released projections today showing that the federal budget surpluses. . . .

THE INCREDIBLE SHRINKING SURPLUS

Editorial Desk (NYT August 24, 2001)
The surplus seems to have vanished while Washington is on vacation. . . .

* * *

STUDY IN CONGRESS SEES NEED TO TAP SOCIAL SECURITY

By Philip Shenon (NYT August 28, 2001)

Congressional budget analysts warned in a report made public today that the economic downturn and President Bush's tax-cut package would force the fed. . . .

TAPPING SOCIAL SECURITY TAXES IS CALLED LIKELY

By Glenn Kessler (WP August 28, 2001)

The federal government is on target to spend billions of dollars in payroll taxes collected for Social Security on other government programs during the rest of President Bush's term, according to a pessimistic congressional report that foreshadows fierce battles over how to allocate the nation's dwindling budget surplus. . . .

SHRINKING SURPLUS MAY FORCE CUTS IN SPENDING

By Glenn Kessler and Dan Morgan (WP August 29, 2001)

The shrinking federal budget surplus has imperiled congressional spending plans, with President Bush's midsummer request for $18 billion in additional defense money the most likely target. . . .

DOMENICI FAVORS TAPPING SOCIAL SECURITY SURPLUS

By Dan Balz and Dan Morgan (WP September 7, 2001)

Sen. Pete V. Domenici (R-NM) the top Republican on the Senate Budget Committee, broke ranks with his party yesterday over the politically sensitive issue of the Social Security surplus, saying that he saw "no reason in the world" why those funds should not be used. . . .

MAJORITY HOLD BUSH RESPONSIBLE FOR DWINDLING SURPLUS

By Dan Balz and Richard Morin (WP September 11, 2001)

A majority of Americans say they are prepared to roll back President Bush's $1.35 trillion tax cut to help deal with the shrinking federal budget surplus and say Bush more than congressional Democrats bears responsibility for a problem that has suddenly put him on the defensive according to a new *Washington Post*-ABC News national survey.

The economy would almost certainly have dominated the news throughout the Bush administration had war not been a preemptive factor. Bush doused consumer confidence on February 8, 2001, when he said, "A warning light is flashing on the dashboard of our economy. And we can't just drive on and hope for the best. We must act without delay." This was part of his sales pitch to get his large tax-cut proposal passed. Bush had been in office less than three weeks at the time, and he was already alarming people about the economy as a political strategy to get legislation through Congress. Bush had inherited from the Clinton administration an economy that was booming, with the lowest level of unemployment in 30 years. Consumer confidence was high, and people were still spending at a rapid pace. There is no way to quantify just how great an impact Bush's gloomy words had on consumer confidence, and thus the recession, but they definitely did have a negative effect.

Bush argued that swift passage of his tax cut could make the difference between growth and recession. But even though his tax cut was passed, the economy continued to be weak. So in 2003, he came back to Congress with the same story that another big tax cut benefiting primarily the rich was needed to jump-start the economy and create jobs.

Bush's credibility on the economy is in big trouble with the American people. He shoved both of his big tax cuts down people's throats without strong majority support. He created a situation which is bound to periodically produce bad economic news for years to come. I do not see consumer confidence returning to the level it was at the end of the Clinton administration anytime soon, and without strong consumer confidence the economy will remain sluggish indefinitely.

The artificially-high interest rates crisis may seem remote to some given the fact that interest rates today are lower than they have been in more than 40 years. But this is a temporary phenomenon. Interest rates tend to fluctuate a great deal over the long run, and this just happens to be one of those times when they are low. As the deficits become larger and larger and the government has to borrow more and more money to cover those deficits and to service the huge national debt, interest rates will be forced up.

Table 7 shows just how much interest rates have fluctuated in the past. It shows the prime interest rate at five-year intervals for the period 1960-2000 and the rate for 2003. The prime rate is the interest rate that large city banks charge their best, low-risk customers. Most borrowers must pay rates that are higher than the prime rate.

The rates in Table 7 range from a low of 4.00 percent for 2003 to a high of 21.50 percent in 1980. Note that in 1960, the prime rate was only 4.50 percent. Many people at that time probably thought that high interest rates would never come back. But come back they did—with a vengeance. In 1981, the prime rate peaked out at an all time record high of 21.5 percent. I remember the unbelievably high interest rates of the 1980s well. Some people thought that they would never again be able to get an affordable home mortgage loan, many building contractors went bankrupt because the high interest rates prevented them from selling the houses they were building, and some bankers just about went crazy with all the uncertainty.

But in the case of interest rates, what goes up usually comes back down, and what comes down usually goes up again. By 1985, the prime rate was down to 9.5 percent, and it stood at 8.5 percent in 1995. In June of 2003 the prime rate was down to 4.00 percent and, just like in 1960, some people were beginning to fall into the mental trap of thinking that low interest rates were here to stay. But they were wrong. The current low interest rates are a temporary phenomenon. Interest rates would be certain to go up again, even if the government ran a balanced budget every year. However, the financing of the huge budget deficits will cause interest rates to rise substantially higher than they would rise in the absence of the deficits.

In addition, as the federal government borrows a larger and larger portion of national savings (the funds that are available for making loans) to fund the deficits and the debt, there will be a smaller portion available for private investment. Because of the shortage of funds that can be borrowed at low enough interest rates to make investment projects profitable, businesses will invest less in new factories and in new technology. In the long run, this means a lower standard of living.

The current position of many leading Republicans is that deficits don't matter all that much. Deficits do matter enormously, and it used to be the Republicans who were the most outspoken critics of deficits.

In a speech on July 19, 1982, at a rally supporting a proposal for a Constitutional Amendment for a Balanced Federal Budget, Ronald Reagan quoted Thomas Jefferson on the subject of the dangers of the public debt as follows:

> Crisis is a much abused word today. But can we deny that we face a crisis? Thomas Jefferson warned, "The public debt is the greatest of dangers to be feared." He (Jefferson) believed that it was wrong and immoral for one generation to forever burden the generations yet to come. His philosophy prevailed for the first 150 years of our history.

TABLE: 7: PRIME INTEREST RATE FOR SELECTED YEARS 1960-2003					
Year	Prime Interest Rate and Date That Rate Became Effective (Percent)				
1960	4.50	08-23-60	1985	9.50	06-18-85
1965	5.00	12-06-65	1990	10.00	01-08-90
1970	8.00	03-25-70	1995	8.50	12-20-95
1975	10.00	01-13-75	2000	9.50	05-17-00
1980	21.50	12-19-80	2003	4.00	06-27-03

Source: Federal Reserve Bank of Saint Louis

Reagan preached the virtue of having balanced budgets throughout his presidency. He even advocated a Constitutional amendment that would force future presidents to balance their budgets. The problem was that Reagan never practiced what he preached. He doubled the national debt during his first 5 years as president, and he and Bush together quadrupled the debt during their 12 years in office.

George Herbert Walker Bush also talked the talk of balanced budgets, but he never walked the walk. In a nationally televised speech to the nation on the evening of October 2, 1990, President George Bush emphasized just how bad and wrong budget deficits are. Excerpts from the President's speech follow.

* * *

Tonight, I want to talk to you about a problem that has lingered and dogged and vexed this country for far too long: the federal budget deficit . . . As we speak, our nation is standing together against Saddam Hussein's aggression. But here at home, there is another threat, a cancer gnawing away at our nation's health. That cancer is the budget deficit. Year after year, it mortgages the future of our children.

No family, no nation, can continue to do business the way the federal government has been operating and survive. When you get a bill, that bill must be paid, and when you write a check, you're supposed to have money in the bank. But if you don't obey these simple rules of common sense, there is a price to pay. But for too long, the nation's business in Washington has been conducted as if these basic rules did not apply. Well, these rules do apply. And if we fail to act, next year alone we will face a federal budget deficit of more than $300 billion, a deficit that could weaken our economy further and cost us thousands of precious jobs. . . .

During his eight years as Reagan's vice president, and during his four years as president, George Bush was directly involved in increasing the national debt from less than $1 trillion to more than $4 trillion.

How could Presidents Reagan and Bush pretend to be so against budget deficits at the same time that they were giving the American public an assembly line of them? How could they preach the evils of budget deficits while at the very time they were pursuing policies that created such large ones and so many of them?

However one answers the preceding questions, it is quite clear that the American people were so fed up with the Reagan-Bush team that they elected a little-known governor from Arkansas to clean up the mess they had made. And Bill Clinton did a pretty good job of cleaning up after Reagan and Bush and putting the government's house back in order.

By listening to the advice of professional economists and pursuing sound economic policies, Clinton played a major role in giving America a second chance to put the federal budget and the national economy back on a sound footing. But America blew that second chance by electing George W. Bush president in the controversial 2000 election.

Even George W. Bush, the king of deficit spending, has spoken at times about how wrong it is for America to burden future generations with a large national debt, such as in his first State of the Union address to the nation on February 27, 2001. Yet, George W. Bush has not paid down a penny of the debt. On the contrary, the national debt is now skyrocketing at a faster pace than ever before. . . .

Deficits and the national debt are critical problems that cannot simply be ignored. Over the long run, deficits lower future economic growth by reducing the level of national savings that can be devoted to productive investments. They also raise interest rates higher than they would be without the deficits, and they raise interest payments on the national debt.

Alan Greenspan warned about the dangers of ongoing deficits in testimony before the House Financial Services Committee on July 16, 2003. An Associated Press article by Martin Crutsinger excerpted the following from his testimony:

There is no question that if you run substantial and excessive deficits over time you are draining savings from the private sector . . . There is no question that we need to come to grips with this deficit question.

Greenspan's statements came just two days after the Bush administration released figures which forecast a record deficit of $455 billion for fiscal 2003. As usual, the deficit figures released were masked by subtracting the temporary Social Security surplus from the on-budget deficit which was estimated to be more than $600 billion.

We, the citizens of the United States, are already paying approximately $1 billion per day in interest on the national debt at a time when interest rates are at a 40-year low. Both future deficits, and increases in the interest rate, will cause that number to escalate rapidly. For example, if interest rates double, the daily interest cost on the debt would rise to $2 billion per day even without any increase in the size of the debt. But we are bound to face both higher interest rates and a rapidly escalating national debt. Without question, interest payments on the national debt will soon once again become the largest expenditure item in the budget, and it will continue to grow more rapidly than any other item with the possible exception of national defense.

What do we Americans get for the $1 billion per day that we currently pay for interest on the national debt? Just think how much it could buy in the form of education, health care, and medical research. Anyone who has a home mortgage knows that, during the early years of the mortgage, most of the payment goes for interest, with only a small portion going toward principle reduction. It is frustrating for homeowners to pay such high mortgage payments and see so little reduction in their debt, but at least there is some reduction in the principle.

With the national debt, even though taxpayers are shelling out such massive amounts in interest payments, the debt is not coming down at all. Instead, it is soaring as our government runs larger and larger deficits.

THE CRISIS OF SOCIAL SECURITY INSOLVENCY is probably the most serious of all problems that we face over the long run. It is not an immediate crisis, but the longer we go without taking action to begin resolving the problem, the more difficult it becomes.

The official version of the Social Security problem, which we receive every year in the form of the annual report of the Social Security Trustees, greatly understates the true severity of it. According to the 2003 Trustees Report, the Social Security fund will continue to take in more revenue than it pays out each year until 2018. However, every year after 2018, the benefit payments due will be larger than the revenue. In other words, there will not be enough revenue to pay for all claims, and the size of the annual Social Security deficit will get larger and larger with each passing year.

What happens after 2018, according to the official version, is that the fund will have to begin dipping into its reserves from all those Social Security surplus years after the 1983 tax increase—enacted, let us remember, to prepare for the retirement of the baby boom generation. The only catch is that all that money has been embezzled and spent for other things by greedy politicians who have engaged in fraud for many years. *There is not a single dollar of cash in the reserves.*

There are, however, lots of government IOUs. The problem is that these IOUs are not marketable. They are simply bookkeeping entries that say that one part of the government (the Treasury) owes the money to another part of the government (the Social Security trust fund). But where is the Treasury going to get all that money it needs to repay its debts to the Social Security trust fund? The Treasury, itself, does not have taxing power. If it is to get the money through higher taxes, it will have to rely on the greedy politicians to levy new taxes on their constituents so money that was fraudulently taken from the trust fund in the past, can be paid back. Just how many members of Congress are likely to voluntarily risk having their angry constituents throw them out of office because they voted for higher taxes?

Of course, by passing huge increases in the debt ceiling, the government could borrow the money to pay off its debts to Social Security, causing the debt, interest rates, and interest payments to go soaring out of sight. The only other option would be for the government to tell the people that it is sorry that there is not enough money to pay full benefits, and then proceed to cut benefits to the level of revenue.

Let's dream a little and make the assumption that the government gets religion and decides to come up with the funds to pay back all the money it owes the Social Security fund. Does that get us out of the woods? Only for a short time.

In the year 2042, even if the government will have paid back every penny it owes to the Social Security trust fund, the fund will be broke, in the sense that it will have no reserves left. It will still be receiving the annual revenue generated by the Social Security payroll tax, but that won't be nearly enough to cover the benefits it owes. It is estimated that during the first year after the fund goes broke in 2042 the revenue would be only about enough to pay 72 percent of benefits due. This would mean that, in 2042, Social Security recipients would get only about 72 percent of what they had gotten the previous year and are legally entitled to in 2042. Each year after that, Social Security would be able to pay a smaller and smaller percentage of the benefits due. Life expectancy continues to creep up, and the number of baby boomers is so large that even if the Social Security fund got back all the money it has loaned to the Treasury, it still would not have enough revenue to pay all the benefits that will be due.

So the Social Security program has two basic problems. One is that the Social Security system, as we currently know it, cannot be sustained over the long run. Even if the government had never misused the Social Security money, there would still not be enough revenue generated by the Social Security tax to pay full benefits after 2042. The number of retirees at that time will just be too large for the fund to remain solvent without reforms. That is the long-term problem that must be addressed long before the fund becomes insolvent.

The shorter-term problem is the direct result of government fraud. If the government had not "borrowed" and spent the Social Security surpluses during the years that followed the 1983 tax increase, there would be no short-term problem. In this event, when the Social Security revenue became insufficient to pay full benefits in 2018, the Trustees would have just dipped into its accumulated reserves to make up the difference, so the program could continue until 2042 when it would face the real problem of having insufficient funds to pay benefits due.

But the government did borrow, or more accurately, embezzle, every dollar of the planned surpluses resulting from the 1983 Social Security tax increase. If something similar to this had happened in a private company or nonprofit charity, many heads would have rolled. It is almost unthinkable that so many government leaders could have participated in this fraud for so many years, including Presidents George Bush, Bill Clinton, and George W. Bush.

Every member of Congress who voted to misappropriate the funds is equally guilty. In my mind, this is a greater scandal than Teapot Dome, Watergate, and all the other infamous U.S. government scandals in history combined. The vast majority of government officials, over a period of many years, participated in this scam, although a few, such as Senator Daniel Patrick Moynihan and Senator Ernest (Fritz) Hollings fought the abuses from the very beginning.

It will have a negative impact on millions of Americans. How severe that impact will be is not yet known. It is my fear that millions of Americans who have faithfully made their contributions to the Social Security fund over many years will be denied part, or all, of the benefits due them. At this point, it seems most likely to me that Social Security as we know it today will not even exist by 2042.

I think the most likely scenario is that the Social Security program will eventually be converted into a means-tested welfare program, and benefits will be available only to the poor. Those who don't qualify under the new rules may receive partial refunds, in the form of monthly installments, of the money they have contributed to the Social Security fund. This is, of course, only my opinion of what is most likely to happen. Only time will tell how this whole problem will play out. The important point is that we are in this predicament only because of the extensive and unforgivable fraud of so many government officials.

Twenty years ago, I could not have even imagined our government defaulting on its future obligations. But then I could also not have imagined our government ever allowing itself to get into such a financial bind as it is in now. Throughout the Reagan-Bush years, as an economist, I could hardly believe what was taking place. How could the American people allow such damage to our economy and budget to continue?

I became personally involved. I wrote a self-syndicated newspaper column on the economy called "Economic Alert." I felt that somebody had to do something, so I began warning my readers on a weekly basis about the disastrous path the nation was following.

In recently reviewing some of my columns, written more than a decade ago, I found one written in 1990 that is just as current now as it was then. It dealt with the Social Security fraud that is still plaguing the nation today, at a time when that fraud was still in its infancy. The following is a reproduction of the column as it appeared in the *Denver Post* on March 5, 1990.

THE DENVER POST   Monday, March 5, 1990
VIEWPOINT: Has the Social Security Trust Fund Been Mismanaged?
Current practices both deceptive and dangerous
By Allen W. Smith

Sen. Daniel Patrick Moynihan of New York sent political and economic shock waves throughout Washington and much of the nation with his proposal to cut Social Security taxes. Although his proposal has received support from the conservative Heritage Foundation, the liberal Institute of Policy Studies and the U.S. Chamber of Commerce, it is strongly opposed by the Bush administration.

"It is an effort to get me to raise taxes on the American people by the charade of cutting them, or cut benefits," Bush told reporters. "And I am not going to do it to the older people of this country."

The controversy goes much deeper than the question of whether to cut Social Security taxes. It involves alleged mismanagement of the Social Security Trust Fund and charges that deceptive accounting practices are understating the size of the Federal Budget Deficit by more than $50 billion per year.

The controversy dates back to 1983 when measures were adopted to build up the Social Security Trust Fund in order to meet soaring benefit costs that will occur when the baby boom generation begins reaching retirement age 20 years from now.

Senator Moynihan was a strong supporter of the 1983 efforts to strengthen the Social Security system. He served on the commission that recommended the plan that involved gradually raising the Social Security tax rate from 6.7 percent in 1983 to 7.65 percent in 1990, and raising the tax base from $35,700 in 1983 to $51,300 in 1990. The latest increase, which went into effect Jan. 1, raised Social Security taxes by $320 a year for people earning $51,300 or more.

The problem is that, instead of being used to build up the size of the Social Security Trust Fund for future retirees as was intended, the surplus in the Social Security fund is being used to pay for general government spending by investing it in Treasury securities.

This practice masks the true size of the federal budget deficit. The projected federal budget deficit for this year is being reported as $141 billion. This official measure of the deficit is $65 billion below the real projected deficit of $206 billion. The government is deducting an expected $65 billion surplus in the Social Security Trust Fund from the real expected deficit (the difference between total federal spending and revenue from all sources except Social Security).

The real deficit for fiscal 1989 was also above $200 billion, but was reported as much less because of last year's $55 billion surplus in the Social Security fund.

The current surpluses in the Trust Fund were supposed to be set aside to build up the fund which will face staggering obligations when the baby boom generation begins retiring about 2010.

Instead, the surplus Social Security money is being used to finance current government spending programs. Outraged by this practice,

Senator Moynihan proposes cutting Social Security taxes and returning the system to a "pay-as-you-go" basis which will provide only
enough revenue to take care of current retirees.

If the government can't keep its hand out of the Social Security
cookie jar, Senator Moynihan wants the cookie jar emptied so there is
no Social Security surplus.

Current government practices are dangerous on two counts. First,
by masking the size of the federal budget deficit, the government is
misleading the American people and giving the impression that the
deficit problem is less serious than it actually is.

Contrary to popular belief, the federal budget deficit has not been
steadily declining in recent years. The on-budget deficit (the difference
between total federal spending and total revenue, excluding Social
Security contributions) was $169.3 billion in fiscal 1987, $193.9 billion in fiscal 1988, and more than $200 billion in fiscal 1989. The idea
that the budget deficit problem is improving is a cruel hoax.

The second major misconception is that the Social Security system,
that was supposedly repaired seven years ago, is currently actuarially
sound for the long term.

At the moment, the Social Security surplus exists only on paper.
The actual funds have been used to help finance the day-to-day operations of the federal government . The funds have been replaced with
Treasury certificates that offer only a pledge that the government will
fulfill its obligations to future retirees by somehow raising the money
in the future.

Current practices are both deceptive and dangerous.
Copyright 1990 Allen W. Smith

As the economic malpractice continued undeterred, I felt com-
pelled to do something more than just write about the problem. I
drafted a proposal for the creation of a National Economic Advisory
Council that would serve as a watchdog for the American people to
ensure that sound economic policies were followed. I met with my
congressman and urged him to introduce legislation for the creation

of such a council. I expressed a desire for him to communicate the proposal to Senator Daniel Moynihan to see if he might be interested in sponsoring such legislation in the Senate.

Not much came of my proposal, but my congressman did at least refer to it on the floor of the House, and have it inserted into the Congressional Record. The following is from the Congressional Record, July 31, 1990, page E2561.

ECONOMIC ADVISORY COUNCIL
HON. TERRY L. BRUCE
OF ILLINOIS
IN THE HOUSE OF REPRESENTATIVES
Tuesday July 31, 1990

Mr. BRUCE: Mr. Speaker, Dr. Allen Smith of Eastern Illinois University in Charleston, IL, has written an excellent column proposing a national economic advisory council. I ask that it be put in the CONGRESSIONAL RECORD, and I urge my colleagues to give it careful consideration. His message is something all of us should ponder.

UNDERSTANDING ECONOMICS No. 28
(By Allen Smith)
THE NEED FOR A NATIONAL ECONOMIC
ADVISORY COUNCIL

In an effort to get the economy out of its current mess and prevent economic malpractice in the future, I propose the creation of a nonpartisan national economic advisory council made up of nine of the best economists in America. The council members, who would serve nine-year staggered terms, would be appointed by the President and confirmed by Congress.

Council members would be ineligible for reappointment so they could remain independent of partisan politics. Since it is essential that council members have a strong grasp of basic economics, only professionally trained economists would be eligible to serve on the council. The council would have only advisory powers, but it would be mandated by law to issue periodic public reports on the state of the economy and on economic policy.

The purpose of such a council would be to serve as a watchdog for the American people to ensure that sound economic policies are followed. Sound economic policy is not Republican, Democratic, conservative, or liberal policy. It is policy based on basic economic principles which are supported by the majority of professionally trained economists. Like members of any other profession, economists disagree on certain aspects of economic policy, however there are many fundamental principles of economics upon which most economists agree. It is some of these most basic fundamental principles that have been ignored in recent years.

This proposal will be about as popular with most politicians as a bad toothache. But if enough Americans supported such a proposal it could be enacted into law. Since members of the council would be appointed, and ineligible for reappointment, they could put the interest of the economy and the American people ahead of any partisan political goals. They would be free to openly disagree with the President and Congress, and they would be obligated to report economic malpractice to the public.

Since the council would have only advisory powers, it could not prevent all economic malpractice or ensure sound economic policy at all times. But, since it would be free to criticize government economic policies without fear of reprisals, it would tend to force the government to pursue responsible economic policies. It would also ensure that professional economists have advisory input into national economic policy.

The actual structure and functioning of any such economic advisory council could differ substantially from my proposal. The important thing is that the American people need a group of highly competent economists who are looking out for the public interests instead of the interests of partisan politicians. Such a council would also benefit the many government officials who have had little or no formal training in the subject of economics. These officials cannot formulate sound economic policies without the advice of competent economists.

Since members of the President's Council of Economic Advisers are selected on the basis of their compatibility with the President's political goals, they serve the political interests of the President which are not always compatible with sound economic policies. The American people need a council of nonpartisan competent professional economists who are mandated by law to promote economic policies that will best serve the long-term interests of the American economy and the American people.

I have already met privately with a member of the U.S. Congress to discuss the feasibility of creating such a council. He is testing reaction to the proposal in Washington, and he may draft a bill proposing legislation that would create such a council. Enacting such legislation will require massive support from the general public. Politicians will not take the initiative in creating a council that would serve as a watchdog for the American people to ensure that politicians put the interests of the American economy above their own political interests. Such legislation will be possible only if the American people demand it. If you support the creation of a nonpartisan national economic advisory council, please send copies of this column, along with your letters of support, to your elected representatives in Washington. We must do more than talk about the need for sound economic policies. We must take action to ensure that they become a reality. Our future, and the future of our children and grandchildren is at stake.

I am even more convinced today than I was thirteen years ago that the American people need some kind of independent committee or council of competent economists to monitor economic policies and blow the whistle on politicians who put personal political interests above the interests of the economy and the people. The specific provisions of the proposal could be altered in various ways and still serve the same purpose. The important thing is to have competent economists monitoring economic policies and reporting economic malpractice to the public at large.

CHAPTER ELEVEN

Pathway To
Economic Disaster

∼

The discussion is are we as a country violating a trust by spending Social Security trust fund moneys for some purpose other than for which they were intended. The obvious answer is yes . . . I think that is a very good illustration of what I was talking about, embezzlement, thievery. Because that, Mr. President, is what we are talking about here. But for the dialog started by the Senator from New York, we would not be here today. And I publicly commend and applaud the vigorous activity generated by the Senator from New York because on that chart in emblazoned red letters is what has been taking place here, embezzlement. During the period of growth we have had during the past 10 years, the growth has been from two sources. One, a large credit card with no limits on it, and, two, we have been stealing money from the Social Security recipients of this country. . . .

—Senator Harry Reid (D-NV) Speech on Senate Floor,
October 9, 1990

I HAVE BEEN FOLLOWING THE economy and the federal budget closely for more than a quarter century. My first book, *Understanding Inflation and Unemployment,* which was published in 1976, resulted from my frustration with the simultaneous high inflation and high unemployment at the time, which could have been avoided with responsible economic policies. As I reflected on the economic policy errors of the Johnson administration, which led to years of unnecessary inflation, and then ultimately to both high inflation and high unemployment, I began to see the enormous damage that one man could do to a national economy and to the lives of millions of people through irresponsible economic policy.

I later coined the phrase "economic malpractice" to describe the actions of political leaders who knowingly and deliberately violate basic economic principles when following the dictates of the principles is not compatible with their current political agendas. It is parallel to the concept of medical malpractice, the accusation that, by violating standard and generally accepted medical practices and procedures, a physician has treated a patient in a way that caused the patient harm and undue suffering.

Although most of our earlier presidents at times pursued economic policies that were inconsistent with sound economics, based on our current knowledge, it was often due more to an overall lack of knowledge about the economy than to a desire to circumvent the principles of economics. It was not until the publication of the monumental book, *The General Theory of Employment, Interest, and Money* by the brilliant British economist John Maynard Keynes in 1935, that a general understanding of how the economy works, and how government actions can harm or help the economy, began to emerge. Therefore, presidents prior to that time can be excused somewhat for practicing unsound economic policies.

John F. Kennedy was the first American president to apply modern economics to his policy decisions. Upon Kennedy's assassination, Lyndon Johnson inherited Kennedy's economic advisers. The problem was that Johnson would follow the advice of the economists when it was politically convenient to do so, but ignore it when it conflicted with his political objectives. Thus, Johnson became the first president to flagrantly engage in economic malpractice.

But then, America paid a terrible price for President Johnson's economic malpractice. In 1965 the economy was in one of its best states ever. It was the seventh year in a row that the inflation rate had remained below 2 percent, and the unemployment rate was at its lowest level in 8 years. Overall, the economy was just about as good as it was possible for it to be. And then we blew it!

Johnson heeded his political advisors rather than his economic experts. With no tax increase to offset the escalation of spending on the war, total spending rose above the full-employment capacity of the economy. With total spending exceeding the capacity of the economy to produce, prices began to rise, and the nation embarked on a long journey of traditional demand-pull inflation. Had the recommended tax increase been implemented, it would have helped to avoid deficits in the federal budget at a time of full employment, and it would also have reduced the after-tax incomes of consumers, which would have caused them to decrease their current spending. It would have been just the opposite of a tax cut targeted at consumers and designed to stimulate increased consumer spending.

Johnson's lack of action to avert the terrible inflation was outrageous and unforgivable. The damage had already been done, but I naively assumed that we at least would never again see such serious economic malpractice. So much had been learned about the economy that, surely, future presidents would listen to the advice of top economists and act on that advice. I couldn't see any reason why they would not.

Nixon, Ford, and Carter had their share of economic problems, but essentially, they listened to their economic advisers and followed fairly sound economic policies. It was not until the election of Ronald Reagan in 1980 that economists were once again shut out of the economic decision-making process, and economic malpractice became the order of the day. Americans should have gotten at least some indication of how radical Reagan's economic proposals were when George Bush, when he was a candidate for the Republican presidential nomination, referred to Reagan's proposals as "voodoo economics" that would lead to disaster if implemented.

I have already given substantial coverage to Reaganomics in earlier chapters. The only part that I want to repeat for emphasis at this point is the fact that people who had never formally studied the subject of economics were allowed to design economic policies over the protests of economists both inside and outside the administration. Budget Director David Stockman, who had never taken even an introductory course in economics, became the chief architect of Reaganomics. Stockman concluded that he knew more about economics than those who had dedicated their lives to the study of the field, including Nobel Laureate Paul Samuelson, and proceeded on a course of experimental economic policy that would have devastating effects on the economy and the American people for decades to come.

Many had hoped that when George Bush became president, he would abandon Reaganomics and chart a new economic course for America. But they were to be disappointed. The nation would have to wait another four years and watch the economy and the federal budget deteriorate further before mainstream, competent economists would again be able to help guide the economy under President Bill Clinton.

Extensive coverage has already been given to the Clinton economic policies and record. Suffice it to say at this point that, when Clinton left office and turned the reins of government over to George W. Bush, the economy was in great shape.

Once again, America had the opportunity to build on a sound economy as it moved forward and tried to resolve the problems of past economic malpractice. The debt was high, Social Security was still in trouble, but those horrible massive deficits were gone—at least temporarily. After eliminating the deficits, Clinton had managed to deliver two years of the first true budget surpluses in 40 years. The economy was at an even better point than it was in 1965 when Lyndon Johnson blew it for political reasons. Surely, America would not blow it again. But we did!

How could American voters have elected a disciple of Ronald Reagan and a son of George Bush as the steward of their future? Didn't we learn anything from the 12 years of Reagan-Bush, as compared to the eight years of Bill Clinton, in terms of the proper management of the economy and the federal budget? Is there anyone, other than the rich and privileged, who can truthfully say they were better off under Reagan-Bush than under Bill Clinton?

Of course, nobody could have known for sure that George W. Bush would be so much more dangerous to America's future than either his father or Ronald Reagan. Yet there was so much reason to believe that his policies would be similar to those of the Reagan-Bush team. It just does not make sense that, of all of the capable Americans available, our nation would entrust our future to a man who at age 40 had never served in any public office, and who had failed at the one business venture he had tried—a man who had been unable to meet the admission standards of the University of Texas Law School.

How could it have happened? Why are we as a nation in the terrible situation we are in today? Why is George W. Bush assaulting the federal budget and the economy with such vigor and determination? Why are more of the American people not angry and outraged that George W. Bush would in two years destroy all the economic progress made during the previous eight years?

Many Ph. D. dissertations in the fields of history and political science will undoubtedly be devoted to these questions for decades to come. Historians will debate why the events of 2000 and later came to be. And the era of George W. Bush will be the focal point of American studies by foreign students.

How is it possible that in the twenty-first century, when the quality of credentials demanded of candidates for all job openings is higher than ever before, that a man with probably the poorest credentials of any president in the history of the nation could become the leader of the free world? How can it be that, no matter what the circumstances of his journey to the White House, George W. Bush would try so hard to destroy the sound economic and budgetary progress made by his predecessor instead of trying to build on it?

These questions seem almost impossible to answer. All that anyone can do is to examine the record and give an educated opinion as to why he or she thinks these things were allowed to happen. I do just that in the remainder of this chapter.

Even if one has no problems with how Bush became president, there is still the huge question of why he seems so determined to bankrupt the nation with his huge unaffordable tax cuts. Bush is not the brightest man ever to occupy the White House, but he is certainly bright enough to know that his tax cuts pose great dangers for America's future. He also knows that his tax policies benefit the rich at the expense of the poor and middle class. That fact is not in dispute, there is clear statistical evidence that proves it. The only thing in dispute is whether there is any justification for widening the gap between the rich and the poor.

There is also no dispute over the position of the vast majority of professional economists on the Bush tax cuts. They oppose them and fear that the cuts will inflict major damage to the American economy and the federal budget. Why would George W. Bush ignore the advice of the top economists in the nation, including ten Nobel Laureates? Would he also ignore the advice of the majority of experts in the field of medicine? Would he turn a deaf ear to the majority of military experts in the Pentagon?

Why must millions of Americans have to suffer the consequences of Bush's economic malpractice? Why is he deliberately assaulting the economy and the federal budget? As president, he may have special Constitutional powers to wage war against other countries. But is there anything in the Constitution that would give him the power to deliberately wage war against the American economy or the federal budget?

In Chapter 8, I wrote about the hidden agenda of the Bush presidency. It does not seem to be very hidden anymore. It appears that Bush is trying to create a severe financial train wreck so that he can impose upon the American people his own vision of the proper role of the federal government. Texas is sometimes referred to as the low-tax, low-service state. Apparently George W. Bush intends to impose his low-tax, low-service philosophy on all of the American people, whether they want it or not. He is trying to starve the government into turning its back on responsibilities it has held for decades.

Since Ronald Reagan became president in January 1981, conservatives have tried to destroy basic social programs, including what is often referred to as the social safety net. They want the federal government to provide national defense and little else. The conservatives would consider the demise of Social Security, Medicare, and Medicaid cause for celebration, and they are determined to prevent the government from ever creating a national health care system such as that of Canada and most other advanced nations.

Unfortunately for the conservatives, and fortunately for the rest of us, the majority of Americans do not support the cutting of services that help prevent people from falling through the cracks. It is inconsistent with the values of most Americans to allow children to suffer from malnutrition or from the lack of access to medical services. Many of us do not believe that whether a person lives or dies should depend on how much money he or she has. And some of us believe that every American deserves the opportunity to get a good education and have access to health care. Some of us are so radical as to believe that we are all born equal, at least in the eyes of God. And I am one of those extreme radicals who believe that the wealthy should not be allowed to use their wealth to buy political power.

Because there are enough people who are compassionate (in the true sense of the word), the conservatives have been unable to convince the majority of Americans to see things their way. But they are absolutely certain that their way of thinking is the only correct way to think. If they cannot impose their values on America through the democratic process, they will slip it in through the back door.

This is the only explanation that makes any sense to me as to why George W. Bush is so determined to move the nation toward bankruptcy. In the long run, for every dollar of permanent tax cuts, there must be a dollar's worth of service cuts. In the mind of George W. Bush, he is not cutting taxes. He is cutting services. And unless his tax cuts are later repealed, he has already preplanned the cutting of services by nearly $2 trillion! Of course, Bush is not doing this all by himself; he has to get enough conservative members of Congress to vote for the services-cut legislation, but that shouldn't be too difficult.

I share Abraham Lincoln's view of the appropriate role of government in America. Lincoln said, "The government should do for the people only those things that the people cannot do for themselves or cannot do as well for themselves." Certainly national defense fits Lincoln's criterion for one of the things the government should do. But many other things such as public education also fit under Lincoln's umbrella. Some services are in the gray area and there is room for debate on them. That is why the American people should determine through the democratic process what things they want the government to do, and how much they are willing to pay for them.

There is nothing wrong with tax cuts so long as the federal budget is in balance and people are informed of what services they will lose as a result of a tax cut. Bush's tax cuts were sold as unconditional gifts to the American people. Not once did I hear Bush say, "On behalf of your government, I am going to give you back some money in exchange for your giving up certain services that you have become accustomed to." Instead, Bush gave the impression that there were no strings attached. He was playing Santa Claus.

Maybe I'm more suspicious than most people. But when anyone tells me they are going to "give" me some money, red flags pop up all over the place. I immediately try to figure out what they expect to get in return. And when a politician offers to give me some money, I know immediately that he is going to want something in return. But I don't think enough Americans have been asking themselves, "What are the Bush tax cuts going to cost me?" We all know, deep down inside, that there is no free lunch, and that there is no Santa Claus for those of us beyond a certain age. But we so much want to believe in Santa Claus, the tooth fairy, and the Easter bunny, that we sometimes ignore the red flags.

IS IT TOO LATE to avert forthcoming economic disaster and the collapse of Social Security? Perhaps, like a politician, I have to answer yes *and* no. Much of the damage that has already been done is irreversible. The skyrocketing growth in the national debt from $1 trillion when Reagan took office to almost $7 trillion today cannot be reversed. That $6 trillion of additional debt will be with us forever. Our children, grandchildren, and all generations that come after them will have to pay interest on this mammoth debt. Furthermore, future interest payments on the debt will be much higher than current payments because interest rates will not remain indefinitely at current abnormally low levels—the lowest rates in the past 45 years. The $1 billion per day in interest that we are currently paying on the national debt will go up proportionately as rates rise.

However, a radical change in course could halt the ongoing damage and keep the national debt from soaring to new highs. We must begin to handle federal finances the same way that any responsible family or business handles its finances. We must terminate the practice of spending money that we don't have. In other words, we must work toward the goal of having an approximately balanced budget over the long term.

Because of the business cycle it is not possible to have an exactly balanced budget each and every year. During recession years there will inevitably be deficits because of the reduced tax revenue that results when workers are laid off and no longer have much income on which to pay taxes. However, during boom years there should be surpluses to help offset the deficits of the recession years so that over the long run the deficit years are approximately offset by surplus years.

Government spending should not exceed the amount of revenue that would be generated by the tax system if the economy were operating at the full employment level. Spending above and beyond the amount of revenue that would be collected at the full-employment level is reckless and irresponsible. If increased spending is absolutely unavoidable because of an emergency such as a war, special arrangements must be made to finance the war. Either a special, temporary emergency tax must be enacted, or the money must be obtained by cutbacks in other spending programs. George W. Bush has done just the opposite—pushed through large tax cuts at the very time that military spending has soared. The simultaneous enactment of big tax cuts and massive increases in military spending is destructive and ruinous to the country's future.

Not one dollar of the Bush tax cuts was ever affordable because there was never any surplus money with which to finance the cuts. Therefore, the first remedial step should be to repeal all tax cuts enacted during the George W. Bush presidency. This would return the tax system to the revenue-generating capacity that existed when President Clinton left office. That tax system led to diminishing deficits during the first six years of the Clinton administration and small surpluses during the last two years when the economy was booming at the top of the business cycle.

Any negative effects that might occur to the economy from the reduction in demand that could accompany an abrupt repeal of the Bush tax cuts could easily be offset by temporary tax rebates for consumers which would give the economy a short-term lift without reducing the tax base or contributing significantly to future deficits.

This step would at least stop the massive hemorrhaging of the federal budget. However, it would not replace the stolen Social Security money. A temporary surtax could be imposed on the wealthy who benefited most from the tax cuts in order to regain some of the lost Social Security funds. While this may not seem politically feasible, the alternative—Social Security tax rates being increased to replace the money that was embezzled from the 1983 tax increases, (along with new safeguarding legislation that would prevent a repeat of the thievery that took place before)—may be even less palatable, not to mention less equitable. If no corrective action is taken, Social Security benefits will have to be drastically cut in the future.

Once the budget is back on a sound footing, if there are new proposals for tax cuts in the future, we must make sure that for every dollar of tax cut there is a dollar of reduced government spending. Whether taxes are too high or too low is a matter of subjective judgment, and is resolved in the political realm. Likewise, whether or not the government provides too many or too few services is also open to political debate. However, the American people must never again be deceived into thinking they can have tax cuts without offsetting cuts in government spending. Through the democratic process, Americans must decide how many government services they are willing to pay for. Tax rates should be no higher and no lower than what is needed to balance the budget based on a level of government spending that voters have chosen.

Speaking of taxes, I believe it is a misnomer when we speak of Social Security deductions as "taxes," and more useful if we think of them as a kind of insurance premium that we pay so as to build up an account from which benefits may be drawn at a later date. But those accounts can only be current if elected officials are honest custodians of that insurance money. Too often in the past, our congressional representatives and presidents have not been good custodians, instead using the Social Security Trust Fund as a kind of legislative piggy bank. Once we do get our fiscal house back in order, we must also stop the common practice of raiding the Trust Fund to fund current government projects. Hardworking people have a right to expect, without fail, that money they have paid into the system will be there for them down the road, in amounts equivalent to their contributions. With honest budgeting, and elected officials who are conscientious sentinels of the Social Security Trust Fund, we may be able to reverse the disastrous trend that is now looming ahead.

CHAPTER TWELVE

Bush's Contract with America

≈

Unrestrained government spending is a dangerous road to deficits, so we must take a different path. The other choice is to let the American people spend their own money to meet their own needs.

—George W. Bush, [February 27, 2001]

*I*BELIEVE THAT THE TWO large tax cuts enacted since George W. Bush became president represent the greatest fraud in the history of American government. I think they are Bush's version of "a contract with America." The only problem is that he has enticed Americans to sign on to the contract without telling them what it is going to cost them. You don't have to be a lawyer to know that you should never sign a contract until all the details are spelled out in clear, indisputable language. A contract constitutes a very specific agreement between two or more parties and should never be entered into by any party until all parties know exactly what they are agreeing to.

Entering into a contract with some of the blanks not yet filled in is illegal and constitutes blatant fraud. Yet, some con artists specialize in such contracts. They get unsuspecting, trusting people to sign a contract without knowing all the specifics of what they are agreeing to.

The President of the United States has entered into a contract with the citizens of America that is alleged to involve free gifts, from the government to the people, with no strings attached. Probably no politician in the history of the entire world ever gave away anything without expecting something in return. George W. Bush is no exception. I believe there are a lot of strings attached to the tax cuts.

The first tax cut enacted in May of 2001 has been touted as a cut of $1.35 trillion over a ten-year period, and the cut enacted in 2003 is alleged to be in the amount of $350 billion. That adds up to a nominal total of $1.7 trillion. But many analysts argue that the tax cuts will cost the government a great deal more than $1.7 trillion. Whatever the ultimate total cost, $1.7 trillion is a lot of money. Bush implies that the American government is just plain giving that $1.7 trillion to the American people with nothing expected in return.

This concept may be hard for a rich boy like George W. Bush to grasp, but it is literally impossible to give away something that you don't have. And the government certainly doesn't have any $1.7 trillion of excess money stuffed under a mattress somewhere.

So when you get to feeling too good about Bush's tax cuts just go back and look at all the speeches and other public pronouncements he has made on the subject. When you read Bush's words, substitute the words "service cuts" for "tax cuts" everywhere "tax cuts" appears. For example, instead of reading, "I want to give the American people $1.35 trillion in *tax cuts* over the next ten years, read, "I want to give the American people $1.35 trillion in *service cuts*" over the next ten years. Does the promise sound as sweet using the words "service cuts" instead of "tax cuts?"

Now let's go back to the 2000 presidential campaign and correct Bush's English for him with regard to the centerpiece of his campaign. Read the words in parentheses—those that represent Bush's intentions—instead of the italicized words—those that come from his lips.

"The government is taking too much *money* (responsibility for providing services) from the American people. The *money* (responsibility for providing services) does not belong to the government. It belongs to the American people. I want to give that *money* (responsibility for providing services) back to the people where it belongs. We have a huge surplus of government *money* (responsibility for providing services). The government has taken too much from the people. So let's return it to the people where it belongs."

I believe the message we get when we read the words in parentheses—instead of the italicized words—is exactly what was in the heart and mind of President Bush. Since every dollar of tax cuts must mean a dollar of service cuts in the long run, Bush was saying what he meant to say (what Karl Rove told him to say) all along. He wanted to give something back to the American people and Karl Rove had taught him to speak C-code, where C stands for conservative.

Rove had explained to Bush several times that "tax cut" and "service cut" really mean the same thing. But they might be confusing to some people. So to make absolutely sure that the conservatives know what we are saying, we must use C-code. All those people who don't speak C-code might be a little confused, but when they actually get the cuts that we have promised them they will know the difference between a tax and a service.

Karl Rove and George W. had this all planned out even before they launched Bush's campaign for governor of Texas. George W. Bush's father had lost the presidency to that despicable Bill Clinton in 1992. So George W. just had to run for governor in 1994 so he would have a stepping-stone to the White House. Even Karl Rove had doubts that George W. could make it all the way from the position of never having held public office to the White House in just one giant leap. So, to play it safe, George W. should be elected governor before trying for the presidency.

Besides, Texas would be a great place to practice Karl's new plan that they had decided to call compassionate conservatism. Since Texans weren't used to having much in the way of either taxes or services, Texas would be the perfect lab for the experiment. Although they had done so to some extent before, Karl decided that it was now time for

George W. and him to fully combine their mental resources and call the result "Bush's Brain."

It is pretty much common knowledge in America that George W. is not the brightest man ever to run for the presidency of the United States, but it is less well known that Karl Rove may well be the brightest presidential adviser ever to gain the ear and confidence of an American president. The combined mental resources of George W. Bush and Karl Rove are an awesome force, but although Karl seems to do pretty well on his own, it seems that just about every time George W. tries to hoof it alone, he gets himself in trouble. So Karl and George W. stick pretty close together.

At any rate, after George W. Bush "won?" the 2000 race for the White House, he and Karl were ready to put their secret plan into effect. A staff member might have asked them, "Why don't you just be honest with the people and tell them that you are going to make massive cuts in government services?" Bush might have replied, "You can't do what we're planning to do, stupid, without tricking the people." Karl Rove, on the other hand, might have been a little more eloquent and said something like, "In order to give the people vinegar, we have to make them think they are getting honey. By the time you're as experienced in political trickery as I am, such a simple concept as this will be a no-brainer."

Phase I of "Operation Fool-the-People" was launched almost immediately. Bush would never admit it, but there was at least one good thing that his immediate predecessor had done. Bill Clinton had actually lied to the American people about the true status of the federal budget. Clinton had claimed that the budget had a $69 billion surplus in 1998, but that was not true, unless you counted the separate Social Security surplus, which you weren't supposed to do. Actually, the government ran a $30 billion non-Social Security deficit in 1998.

In 1999 and 2000, although there were true non-Social Security surpluses, they were not nearly as large as Clinton claimed. He had added the off-budget Social Security surpluses to the true surpluses for those two years. In addition, Clinton claimed that there were huge budget surpluses for as far as the eye could see. These lies by Clinton were going to make it so much easier for George W. Bush and Karl Rove to pull the wool over the eyes of the American people.

Clinton was not the only one saying there was a surplus. Vice President Al Gore and many other politicians were making the same claim. If it had been true that large budget surpluses had somehow sneaked up on the government while nobody was watching, it would have been a sensational story. Well, journalists, most of whom have little or no training in economics, treated the story as if it were real. And soon almost the entire nation was caught up in the budget-surplus myth.

That being the case, Phase I of Operation-Fool-the-People went very smoothly. How could people be against a tax cut when the government had all that surplus money? In his first State of the Union address, Bush made several points and promises to the American people which, if true, might very well have justified the tax cut.

Of course, it took quite an imagination to envision all that surplus money. According to Bush, there was enough to adequately fund government operations, provide for contingencies, protect the Social Security surplus, pay down an unprecedented amount of our national debt, and then still have money left over.

If George W. Bush had not been president of the United States, it would have been easy to conclude that he was a snake oil salesman. It seemed almost as if he was saying that the United States, through some kind of magic, had tapped a perpetual flow of income. No matter how much they dipped out, there would still always be plenty left over.

Some more sophisticated Americans didn't buy the pitch. They figured that either Bush was crazy, or he was just saying what Karl Rove had told him to say. After all, Karl Rove's imagination was plenty big enough to have envisioned all that money, or to have concocted such an elaborate scheme.

But most Americans soon became very comfortable with George W. as president. He just seemed like one of the guys. He used very simple English most of the time, and sounded a lot like some of the good old boys they knew who hadn't even finished high school. On the other hand, once in a while he would come up with one of those big words that nobody seemed to have ever heard of before. But they figured he must have learned those words at the Harvard Business School.

George W. seemed very trustworthy, and was very religious. He just had to be telling the truth, no matter how much it sounded like a big fish story. And in his State of the Union speech, he had said something about letting, "The American people spend their own money to meet their own needs." So, since there was all that surplus money just sitting in government vaults somewhere, doing nobody any good, if the president wanted to give it to the American people, most thought it was a pretty good idea.

Not long after that first tax cut people began hearing things on the news about the shrinking surplus, the return of budget deficits, dipping into the Social Security surplus, and a lot of people losing their jobs. Then the country went through the terrible times of the terrorist attacks, and most Americans felt relieved that a man like George W. Bush was president and commander in chief. During wartime, everybody is expected to rally behind the president and stop criticizing him, even about domestic issues such as large budget deficits and unemployment. The president became very popular during this time, and the news media didn't cover much news about the economy.

Even before we got through with the war in Afghanistan, President Bush began warning Americans that we might soon have to go to war with Iraq. He said he didn't really want to go to war, but Iraq had weapons of mass destruction that were a threat to the United States and the rest of the world, and Iraq refused to destroy them. As we seemed to be getting closer and closer to war, there appeared to be only one hope for avoiding it. If Iraq disarmed and got rid of its weapons of mass destruction, war could be avoided, according to

Bush. But Iraq insisted that it did not have weapons of mass destruction and therefore could not destroy something it didn't have. Iraq was finally given an ultimatum to destroy, and prove to the world that it had destroyed, all weapons of mass destruction. When it failed to do so, we went to war with Iraq.

As the Iraq war news trailed off, the news media began covering other news stories, including the economy. Americans learned that the results of the 2001 tax cuts were not quite what President Bush had promised. Instead of facing budget surpluses as far as the eye could see, the government was now facing massive deficits far into the future, and more than two million jobs had been lost since Bush became president.

Many analysts recommended repealing the 2001 tax cuts in an effort to reduce the size of the projected budget deficits. But George W. Bush and Karl Rove had other plans. Instead of repealing the tax cuts that had already been enacted, they called for a new round of large tax cuts. This time, the mental resources of both George W. and Karl combined were not sufficient to figure out how to pull off Phase II of Operation Fool-the-People without some basic changes.

The large budget surpluses, they had assured the American people, existed as far as the eye could see, were nowhere to be seen. Phase I of Operation Fool-the-People had been sold to the public on the basis that the government had all that surplus money. The public fell for it the first time, but they couldn't be fooled again in the same way. The problem was that, as before, Bush wanted to give most of the money to the rich with just a few crumbs such as child tax credits thrown in to make the proposal palatable to more people. But that would be a very hard sell with more than two million American workers unemployed. Somehow, they had to find a way to put more emphasis on the compassionate part of compassionate conservatism.

After a little brainstorming, Rove came up with an idea. It had to do with that vinegar vs. honey strategy. If they could make the people believe that the vinegar going to lower and middle income families was really honey in disguise, and still give the real honey to the rich, they just might be able to sell their snake oil to the public. It would be a real challenge, though. George W. and Karl were puzzled as to how so many Americans had figured out so soon that the first round of vinegar was really vinegar instead of honey as George and Karl had claimed.

What they did was tell people that their big tax cut for the rich in the 2003 proposal was really a job creation bill to get all those poor unemployed workers back to work. But it was an even harder sell than they had expected. A bunch of brazen economists took out a full-page ad in the *New York Times* telling the people that it was a tax cut for the rich—not a jobs creation bill. If that weren't bad enough, some of the rank and file Republicans in the Senate refused to be a party to the fraud. It took Vice President Cheney's tie-breaking vote to get the legislation through the Senate, but they got it through.

It was time to celebrate. Both Phase I and II of Operation Fool-the-People had been successfully completed, so Bush's treasured Contract With America was now in force. Unless some wise guy did something to sabotage the whole plan, Bush's service cuts would become reality. Through Operation Fool-the-People, George W., with a lot of help from Karl Rove, had managed to accomplish what both Ronald Reagan and Bush's father had failed to achieve. He had set in motion a plan that would ultimately result in service cuts far beyond anything the American people could have imagined.

George W. was pretty proud of himself. And as he reread the final draft of his first State of the Union speech, he was proud that he had outfoxed the whole nation. Nobody could accuse him of misleading the American people. How could they? He had told them in that very first speech what he was going to do. He had said:

> Unrestrained government spending is a dangerous road to deficits, so we must take a different path. The other choice is to let the American people spend their own money to meet their own needs.

There it was in plain black and white. His goal all along was to let the American people spend their own money to meet their own needs. If some of the people don't have any money to spend, that's not his fault.

The Case For Universal Economic Education

~

*A government resting upon popular suffrage cannot be successful
unless those who elect and who obey their governors are educated.*

—John Dewey

*T*HIS BOOK DESCRIBES HOW political leaders have managed
to knowingly and deliberately inflict great harm on the economy, the federal budget, and the American people over the past two
decades, by pursuing policies that were incompatible with sound principles of economics. During the 12 years of the Reagan-Bush administrations the national debt quadrupled, and by the time George Bush
turned over the powers of the presidency to Bill Clinton in January
1993, the economy and the federal budget were headed for a crash.

Economists, who had seen the calamity coming since the early days
of the Reagan administration, breathed a sigh of relief when George
H.W. Bush was forced to step aside and turn the controls over to
Clinton, but many economists had serious doubts that Clinton could
avert the crash at that late stage of the downward plunge. However,
with the help of a crew made up of some of the most competent economists available, the crash was averted, and the plane known as the
American economy began to recover altitude. If the new pilot had not
been capable of understanding what the economists were saying, or if

he had failed to implement their advice, there is little doubt that the crash would have come on Clinton's watch.

Fortunately, Clinton had a brilliant mind and was able to see the impending crisis. He took the corrective actions recommended by the economists, which included both major spending cuts and a tax increase. He was opposed by every single Republican member of both the House and the Senate, and he managed to get the urgently needed legislation through Congress only with the tie-breaking vote of Vice President Al Gore. Many of Clinton's opponents predicted that his policies would devastate the economy. They argued that the new pilot would crash the plane by following the advice of his trusted economists, especially the advice to raise income taxes. Specifically, Senator Robert Dole said, "To put it simply, the Clinton tax increase promises to turn the American dream into a nightmare for millions of hardworking Americans."

The critics were wrong. The economy responded to the new policies remarkably well. The downward plunge was aborted, and the plane began at first to level off, and then to resume its upward journey once again. Economists were relieved, and soon the skills of the new pilot were publicly recognized by such giants as former Federal Reserve chairman, Paul Volker, and current chairman Alan Greenspan. Both Volker and Greenspan praised Clinton's piloting skills as did many other prominent public figures. It seemed that the only ones who were displeased with the results of Clinton's piloting were the Republicans, who had made a big deal back in 1993 about how they did not want to be held responsible for the consequences of Clinton's economic policies.

Most fair-minded Americans did not hold the Republicans responsible, nor did they give them any credit for the prosperity and diminishing deficits that resulted from Clinton's policies. How could they be held responsible when not a single one of them had voted for the program? Since they could not make any political gains by criticizing his handling of the economy, the Republicans began focusing on Clinton's personal life.

During the first six years of the Clinton presidency, the operating budget (on-budget) remained in negative territory. However, the huge deficits of the Reagan-Bush years would soon be only a terrible memory. Clinton consistently and persistently slashed away at the deficits, year by year, going from the horrible record on-budget deficit of $340.5 billion during the last year of George Bush's admininstration to the first two true budget surpluses in 40 years in 1999 and 2000. Of course, the huge national debt that had accumulated from the large budget deficits of the past remained with us, but at least we were no longer adding to the size of the national debt, now that the deficits had been eliminated.

The American economy was soaring at a high altitude by the end of Clinton's presidency. The economy was in the 10th year of the longest expansion in history, the unemployment rate was at a 30-year low, and we had just experienced the first two years of true budget surpluses in 40 years. In short, the economy was in the best condition in the history of the nation, but it was time for the pilot who had averted the near crash, and now had the economy soaring, to step aside. Since Clinton was no longer eligible to pilot the plane, many economists felt almost sure the job would go to Al Gore, who had been at Clinton's side for eight years and could be counted on to pilot the economy in the exact same way as Clinton had. But as we all know, that did not happen. Instead, at the helm was a student of Reaganomics and the son of the man who had almost crashed the economy before Clinton came along just in the nick of time.

Economists listened to George W. Bush's plan with alarm. He was proposing to undo what had been accomplished during the previous eight years. He was calling for another round of Reaganomics—the policy that had almost caused the economy to crash before Clinton took charge.

The national debt was more than $6 trillion when George W. Bush became president, so it was absolutely shocking when the new pilot proposed additional large cuts in tax rates. The tax rate structure that existed after the Clinton tax increase was unable to generate enough revenue to balance the budget except in those last two Clinton years when the economy was operating at the very top of the business cycle. There had been deficits during 6 of the 8 years that Clinton had occupied the White House, so as soon as the economy slipped into even a minor recession, the nation was bound to experience at least small annual budget deficits under the tax structure that George W. Bush had inherited.

If Bush had left tax rates alone, and worked to cut government spending as much as possible, we might have had almost balanced budgets in the years ahead, and the economy could have continued to prosper. But that was not the route that Bush took. He advocated massive tax cuts. Had he learned nothing from the policies of Reagan and his father!

This new daredevil pilot was preparing to throw the economy back into a nosedive. But how could he? Didn't he realize just how close we had come to crashing before his father was relieved of his duties? And if he did realize the close call America had had before Clinton took office, was he out of his mind to propose another crash attempt? It just didn't make sense to economists, and if the people had understood what George W. was up to, they would probably have refused to support him. But they did not understand.

Bush was masquerading as a person who wanted to do what was best for America and its citizens, so the American people literally trusted him with their lives. Many were concerned that what Bush was proposing lacked the support of most professionally trained economists, but Bush convinced them that he knew more than the economists knew. Most Americans did not have a clue that Bush was lying to them when he made the following statements:

- "My plan pays down an unprecedented amount of our national debt."
- "My budget protects all $2.6 trillion of the Social Security surplus for Social Security and for Social Security alone.
- "And then, when money is still left over, my plan returns it to the people who earned it in the first place."

Even if there had been no tax cuts, there would not have been any money with which to pay down the debt by even one dollar during Bush's four-year term unless he either raised taxes or cut government spending in other areas. Even during the prosperous Clinton years, only during his last year in office, when the economy was at the peak of the business cycle, was there a significant on-budget surplus which could be used to pay down the national debt. There was little likelihood that there would be any non-Social Security surpluses during the next four years, no matter who was serving as president.

And just as there was no money to pay down the debt, there was also not a single dollar available for funding tax cuts. The only way that Bush could have cut taxes without damaging the economy and the budget would have been to cut government spending dollar for dollar by the amount of any tax cut. But this was not what the voters wanted to hear. So Bush chose to tell them that he would pay down the debt, protect Social Security money, and also cut taxes. He knew he was lying to the American people, but it didn't seem to bother him. He knew that his nose would not grow longer the more lies he told. In fact, he didn't think the American people would even know that he was lying.

As I pointed out early in this book, Bill Clinton, Al Gore, and many members of Congress from both parties also lied about the existence of a mythical government surplus. They should also be condemned for their lies, but the fact that others had lied in no way justifies Bush's duplicity. How could the president of the United States blatantly lie to the American people in his State of the Union address about an issue that was so crucial to our economic security? I can't answer that question. All I know is that George W. Bush did lie to the American people about the financial condition of the government in his 2001 State of the Union address, and he has been lying about the economy and the federal budget ever since.

Of all the lies Bush has told, I personally find the lie that the 2003 tax cut was a jobs-creation program the most offensive and the most cruel of all. More than two million Americans lost their jobs between the time of Bush's inauguration and his last-minute campaign to muster enough votes in Congress to pass those tax cuts.

As I stated earlier, 400 of the nation's top economists, including 10 who had won the Nobel prize in economics, were so concerned about the damage the tax cut would do, and about Bush's betrayal of the American people, they took out a full-page ad in the *New York Times* in an effort to get their message to the public. They left no doubt about what they believed the purpose of the bill was in their statement, which follows.

"... Regardless of how one views the specifics of the Bush plan, there is a wide agreement that its purpose is a permanent change in the tax structure and not the creation of jobs and growth in the near-term ... Passing these tax cuts will worsen the long-term budget outlook, adding to the nation's projected chronic deficits ..."

It is hard to understand how any president of the United States could do what Bush did in those last few days before the tax cut was passed. He totally ignored the warnings of these top experts and set out to convince the people that his bill would do just the opposite of what the 400 experts had said it would do. Few people outside New York City were aware of the economists' statement, and Bush wanted to keep it that way. He went on a speaking blitz to drum up votes for passage of his bill. In speech after speech, he referred to the high unemployment in America and claimed that his tax cut was a solution to it. He referred to the bill over and over as a "jobs-creation" program that must be passed in order to solve the problem of high unemployment.

Every time he made that statement, he knew he was deliberately lying to the people who had put so much trust in him. He didn't try to refute the economists' argument that the tax cut would not create many jobs. Instead, he took advantage of the fact that most Americans (outside of New York City) were totally unaware of their warning. Most Americans could not have imagined that the "trustworthy" President George W. Bush would be pushing any kind of legislation that was opposed by the vast majority of experts in the field. Most thought Bush was trying to do something good for them by pushing through legislation that would reduce unemployment.

The nation very much needed a jobs-creation bill at that time, and the cost of a true jobs-creation program would have been only a fraction of the cost of Bush's big tax cut for the rich. For example, a bill that would have provided for the sending of a one-time check of $1,000 to every American taxpayer would have given the economy a real big jolt—perhaps even too big a jolt—but it would not have changed tax rates and would therefore not have contributed significantly to long-term budget deficits. Economists would have gladly supported such a measure with the correct amount of the rebate adjusted to the level that would have provided the appropriate boost to the economy.

Bush could have easily gotten such legislation through and could have made a major contribution toward putting unemployed workers back to work. Instead, he chose to do another big favor for members of his own socioeconomic class—the people who had made possible his presidency and who would finance his reelection campaign. Bush knew that every favor he did for these people would make it easier for him to raise massive amounts of money with which to "buy" a second term. A few weeks after the passage of the 2003 tax cut, Bush raised $7 million in campaign contributions during one weekend in Texas. Such campaign contributions by the wealthy to the first Bush campaign probably yielded a greater return to the donors than any other investment they had ever made.

Instead of paying down the national debt, Bush is increasing it at an alarming rate. Based on the administration's own OMB projections, *Bush will increase the national debt by more during the next two years than was accumulated during the first 200 years* of American history. And there is no end in sight. It appears that there will be on-budget deficits of at least $500 billion ($½ trillion) per year for the indefinite future. And the Social Security trust fund is as empty as ever, at a time when Bush is using the Social Security surpluses to help fund his huge tax cuts for the very rich. George W. Bush now has the economy in such a nosedive that it will be extremely difficult to avoid a crash.

As an economist, I feel very much like a physician must feel when he or she sees a child suffering, and possibly dying, because the parents refuse to allow the child to take modern medication that could help. Actually the economist is in an even more frustrating position than the physician, because the physician can appeal to the courts for help in forcing the parents to allow the child to receive proper health care.

As I mentioned in an earlier chapter, my first book, *Understanding Inflation and Unemployment*, which was published in 1976, was written because of my frustration with President Lyndon B. Johnson's failure to follow sound economic policies to head off the terrible inflation that was set off at least partly by the massive increase in spending on Vietnam without a corresponding increase in taxes. That book marked the beginning of my long crusade for economic education to combat the incredibly dangerous economic illiteracy of the American people.

I was absolutely dumbfounded by Reagan's economic proposals— the ones that George Bush initially called "voodoo economics." I was even more shocked when Reagan's proposals were enacted into law, and America started down the long road toward economic disaster. It was like a huge breath of fresh air when Bill Clinton was elected and began once again implementing sound economic policies. Because of the success of Clinton's policies, and the contrast between the results of his economic policies and those of Ronald Reagan and George Bush, I felt almost sure that major economic malpractice was a thing of the past. Americans could clearly see how different the 12 years under Reagan-Bush were as compared to the 8 years of Clinton when traditional economic policies were again followed. Very few Americans would say that they were better off under Reagan-Bush than under Clinton. There had never been greater economic prosperity in America than during the last two years of the Clinton presidency.

In my mind, it didn't matter all that much whether a Democrat or a Republican succeeded Clinton, because the value of following the advice of highly competent economic advisers had been demonstrated. Surely, even a Republican president would follow sound economic policies, I thought. And I still firmly believe that most of the other Republican candidates for president in 2000 would have followed sound economics policies. Certainly John McCain would have done so.

But, George W. Bush did make it to the White House, and he did follow through with his radical economic policies that were so unthinkable to many economists. He was determined to push through his big tax cuts for the wealthy, come hell or high water, and there was nothing anybody could do to stop him, given the high degree of economic illiteracy in America.

I tried my best to alert people to the dangers ahead. I drove my debtmobile, which was a 1991 red Oldsmobile Cutlass Supreme plastered with warning signs on all sides and on the top, up and down the streets of Miami, Tampa, Tallahassee, and other Florida cities, trying to attract the attention of the news media. Large signs with warnings about the deficits and the national debt, spelled out in large letters so they could easily be read from the air, were mounted on the top of the car. I hoped that helicopters from the news media would spot me and come down for a closer look.

Finally, in September 2001, my efforts to alert the public to the true status of the federal budget seemed to be about to bear fruit. The Associated Press did an article about me, and my crusade for economic education, entitled, "Economist warned of budget surplus myth, now vindicated." Vickie Chachere, the correspondent who wrote the article, told me she thought the story would be picked up by newspapers around the country.

I was hopeful that my efforts would soon pay off as the budget surplus myth, which the Bush administration was still pushing to the hilt, was exposed. I thought it was just a matter of time until the media and the American public would learn that they were being deliberately deceived by their government.

I spoke with Vickie by phone just before the story was to be released to the wires, and I said something like, "I hope there are no major stories that dominate the news and crowd out the other stories." Vickie said she thought things would be relatively quiet and that I needn't worry about the story not receiving wide exposure.

The story appeared on the Florida wire and was about to go national. But, like so many other stories, it was buried by the avalanche of news generated by the events of September 11. To my knowledge, the story, which is reprinted below, never made it to the national wire.

ECONOMIST WARNED OF BUDGET SURPLUS MYTH, NOW VINDICATED
By Vickie Chachere, Associated Press
(Reprinted with permission of The Associated Press)

TAMPA—A year ago, economist Allen W. Smith seemed an oddity, a bespectacled Chicken Little with an ominous warning that the nation's economic outlook wasn't as good as it seemed.

He wrote a book about what he believes is the myth of a federal budget surplus. He even went on CNN to spread his warnings there was no surplus, only a looming national debt.

Still no one seemed to be listening. Smith, a former writer of an economics column and the author of nine books, pressed on.

The election—with its candidates making big promises about how they would use the surplus—came and went, and Smith grew frustrated.

Finally, two months ago, Smith, a Midwesterner not prone to absurd acts, felt moved to plaster signs on his bright red car and drive about town in an elaborate "The End is Near" sort of warning.

Smith's grown children were embarrassed. Some of his neighbors called him a loon.

Then this week came vindication with news the government needs to borrow $9 billion from Social Security reserves to make ends meet, says a new Congressional Budget Office estimate.

"I knew this would happen," said Smith, 63, trying hard not to gloat. "(CNN's) Lou Waters said I was a voice crying in the wilderness, I guess I was. I knew it was just a matter of time."

If it wasn't such a serious issue, it might almost be comical, But for Smith, a professor emeritus at Eastern Illinois University who has long been on a crusade to educate the common folk about the weighty issues of economics, it's more proof that what Americans don't know about economics hurts them.

"It's a deception they (voters) like to hear," he said. "The problem is the economic illiteracy."

For Smith, the lack of understanding about budget surpluses and deficits is a double concern.

Not only does he feel politicians have been misleading people about how such surpluses could be spent on improved health care or education, he worries that people are making poor choices for themselves based on misinformation. He fears a deep, prolonged economic recession is ahead.

"I actually have a very gloomy outlook," Smith said. "I am glad I'm retired and not out in the job market."

Smith's book, *The Alleged Budget Surplus, Social Security & Voodoo Economics*, calls the budget surplus a myth that "may go down in history as the greatest deception perpetrated on the American people."

In the book, written in early spring last year, Smith argued that the economy was healthy, but the federal budget was not.

The bulk of the budget surplus was Social Security Trust Fund money and it wasn't the government's to spend on programs other than paying benefits to those who have paid into the retirement program, he wrote. The book was published in late September.

Using data gleaned from the U.S. Department of the Treasury and other government economic reports, Smith argues in his book that the public was duped into believing there was a surplus and is forgetting $5.7 trillion national debt.

He said the only surpluses were in 1999 and 2000, in the peak of the economic boom, and they were smaller than the public was led to believe, Smith contends.

Smith took to task both Republicans and Democrats in the book, calling their comments about the economy and their campaign promises simply irresponsible.

He does, however, think the recent tax rebates are a good idea for a short-term boost for the economy, if they're spent as President George Bush intends.

Frustrated by the lack of interest in the issue, Smith said he was ready to give up earlier this summer when he had an epiphany while standing in line at a post office.

Soon thereafter, his cherry red 1991 Oldsmobile Cutlass Supreme was transformed into the debt mobile. Smith plastered the car with signs warning of the $1 billion-a-day interest and the mythical surplus and began traveling the state. . . .

All the economic malpractice of the past two decades, and the suffering that has resulted from it, could have been avoided if the American public had been economically literate. But they are not, they are incredibly illiterate on the subject of economics. This applies to highly educated professionals just as much as it does to the general public, and it especially applies to all government officials. I seriously doubt that President Bush, or most members of Congress, could pass a basic economic literacy test. Most Americans have never formally studied economics. Only 13 states require that high school students take a course on basic economics and the American economy. As a result, most high school graduates have never been exposed to the subject. In many of the nation's high schools, economics is not even offered as an elective course for those students who might want to take it.

One of the most powerful actions that our government could take to reduce economic illiteracy, and thus economic malpractice, in the long run would be to ensure that every future high school graduate will have taken a course on the American economy before being allowed to graduate. While the federal government might not have the authority to mandate what is taught in the individual states, it could certainly use the carrot and stick approach. If the government adopted a policy of withholding federal education funds from any school that did not teach a required course on the American economy, almost every high school in the nation would soon be teaching the subject.

The cost of adding a course on the American economy would be minimal for most high schools. Every licensed high school social studies teacher has already had some training in economics, and the National Council on Economic Education, through its local centers for economic education, offers special classes designed to train high school teachers to teach economics. Thirteen states have already shouldered the responsibility of educating students on the American economy. We can't wait decades for the other states to follow in their footsteps. We must take action now to ensure that the next generation will not be as economically illiterate as present ones are.

Requiring every future high school graduate to have taken a course on the American economy is a good starting point, but it is not nearly enough. I believe the government should sponsor free adult night classes at community colleges and local high schools for those members of the general public who would like to learn about the American economy. The federal government has in the past sponsored such programs to reduce overall illiteracy in America. Many Americans have learned the basic skills of reading and writing as adults through such programs.

Some people think that those with a college education surely must know a great deal about the economy as well as most other subjects. Not true. The majority of college graduates are economically illiterate, having made it through college without taking a single course in economics. In most colleges, economics is not a general education requirement. Only students with certain majors are required to take it as part of their college education.

As a result, there are many doctors, lawyers, and other highly educated individuals who have almost no understanding of the American economy. Most members of the United States Congress have probably never had any formal training in economics. Yet they play a major role in the functioning of the economy through the legislation they pass. It is very much like the blind leading the blind. A president, who knows little about economics, proposes basic legislation that will have a major impact on the economy and the future of the American people. An equally illiterate Congress then debates the proposed legislation mostly on political grounds, because they don't know enough to debate the economic aspects of the legislation.

Educators in almost all disciplines think that their discipline should be more widely taught. One person even raised the following question to me. "Why should all students be required to take economics unless they are also required to take chemistry? My answer to this type of argument is that the American voters are rarely called upon to vote on issues that require a good understanding of chemistry. In such fields, we can rely on the experts to keep us on the right track. But every time voters vote, economic issues are involved.

Every high school student gets instruction in both American history and American government, but most do not study the American economy. Yet it is not possible to have a good understanding of either American history or American government without also having a good understanding of the American economy. It may not be necessary for people who live in nondemocratic countries to be educated in economics, since they don't have any say in government policies. But it is absolutely essential that those of us who live in democratic nations have at least some familiarity with economics and the American economy.

When President George W. Bush ignored the warnings of the nation's top economists and pushed through his dangerously irresponsible 2003 tax cut, it removed any remaining doubt that professional economists might have had that they could have any impact on economic policy-making. It is absolutely crucial that we Americans try to protect ourselves, and the nation, against radical economic malpractice by becoming more informed about the American economy.

I urge readers to support universal economics education at the high school level, and to try to persuade colleges and universities to make principles of economics a general education requirement so that at least college graduates will be able to play a role in battling economic malpractice. I also urge readers to support the creation of a national economic advisory council similar to the one I proposed in Chapter 10. The American people need a watchdog agency to protect them from government officials like President George W. Bush who attempt to exploit economic illiteracy in order to further their partisan political agendas.

The Best Friend
Social Security Ever Had

S ENATOR DANIEL PATRICK MOYNIHAN (Dem., NY)
dedicated his life to improving the lives of others. His intellect,
and his emphasis on principle before politics, was a combination rarely
found in elected officials, and it won him the respect and admiration
of people of all political persuasions around the world. Moynihan was
described in the *Almanac of American Politics* as "the nation's best
thinker among politicians since Lincoln and its best politician among
thinkers since Jefferson." ABC News described Moynihan as "larger
than life, provocative, theatrical and brilliant."

In addition to his many productive years in the Senate, Daniel
Patrick Moynihan worked in the U.S. Department of Labor under
Presidents Kennedy and Johnson and served as a special adviser to
President Nixon, as ambassador to India, and as ambassador to the
United Nations.

Moynihan's intense interest, expertise, and efforts to fight government fraud in the Social Security program made him, in my opinion,
the best friend that Social Security ever had. I had hoped to interview
Senator Moynihan while writing the book, because I considered him
the most authoritative elected official in America on the subject of

Social Security. Unfortunately, his unexpected passing in March 2003 made that impossible.

Senator Moynihan served on the 1982 Presidential Commission that was charged with finding ways of dealing with the Social Security crisis that would occur when the baby-boom generation began retiring in 2010. He spearheaded the 1983 legislation that raised Social Security taxes for the purposes of building up a surplus reserve fund in advance of the boomers' retirement. Moynihan was determined to do everything in his power to ensure that future retirees would receive the benefits to which they were entitled.

When President George H. W. Bush used the surplus Social Security funds for general government spending, instead of setting it aside for future retirees, Moynihan was outraged. The issue came to a head in 1990 when Senator Moynihan sent shock waves throughout Washington and much of the nation with his proposal to cut Social Security taxes.

Senator Moynihan, who felt the American people were being betrayed and deceived, proposed undoing the 1983 legislation by cutting Social Security taxes and restoring the "pay-as-you-go" structure that would have provided only enough revenue to take care of current retirees. Moynihan thought it was very dangerous and deceptive for the government to use the surplus in the Social Security trust fund to pay for general government spending, he wanted to cut Social Security taxes so there would be no surplus to mask the enormous deficits in the government's operating budget.

Moynihan continued to fight for the rights of Social Security beneficiaries and for solvency of the trust fund for the rest of his life. His last major contribution toward "making Social Security as solvent as possible" was his serving as co-chair, along with AOL-Time Warner CEO Richard Parsons, of President George W. Bush's President's Commission to Strengthen Social Security in 2001. We are all indebted to Moynihan for his contributions toward making Social Security as solvent as possible. He was a man of principle who stood up for what he believed.

ACKNOWLEDGMENTS

~

*T*HANKS TO CAROL MANN, my agent, and to Philip Turner, Executive Editor at Carroll and Graf Publishers, for recognizing the importance and timeliness of this book early on when it was in the proposal stage. Also, special thanks to Philip for putting the book on the fast track and rushing it to press because of the urgency of its contents.

Thanks to my special friend, Victor Stoltzfus, President Emeritus of Goshen College. Vic has been my sounding board and a major source of encouragement over the past three years as I struggled to find a voice with which to alert the public to the catastrophic policies that were leading the nation down the road to fiscal disaster.

Most of all, I thank my wife, Joan, who read every page of the manuscript from the first draft to the final one and put almost as much heart and soul into the work as I did. Joan is a constant source of inspiration, encouragement, and support in all my writing endeavors.

INDEX

~

ABOUT THE AUTHOR

~

*A*LLEN W. SMITH has been battling economic illiteracy for more than 25 years. His first book, *Understanding Inflation and Unemployment,* became an alternate selection of Fortune Book Club. His high school textbook, *Understanding Economics,* was published ten years later by Random House and was used by more than 600 schools in 48 states. Dr. Smith's other books include *Demystifying Economics: The Book that Makes Economics Accessible to Everyone,* and *The Alleged Budget Surplus, Social Security & Voodoo Economics,* both published in 2000.

From 1990–1993, Smith wrote a syndicated weekly newspaper column on the economy that appeared in 30 newspapers with a combined circulation of one million. He has published articles on the economy in the *Denver Post, Philadelphia Inquirer,* and the *St. Louis Post-Dispatch.* In addition, Smith has been the guest on more than 70 radio talk shows throughout the nation.

Smith taught economics to college students for 30 years, retiring in 1998 as Professor of Economics at Eastern Illinois University to become a full-time writer. He holds a B.S. in Education from Ball State University, Muncie, Indiana, and an M.A. and Ph.D. in Economics from Indiana University, Bloomington, Indiana.

He currently lives in Winter Haven, Florida.